DEAR VONDA KAY

By Vonda Kay Van Dyke

THAT GIRL IN YOUR MIRROR
DEAR VONDA KAY

DEAR VONDA KAY

Former Miss America

Vonda Kay Van Dyke

Answers Questions Teen-agers Ask

FLEMING H. REVELL COMPANY
WESTWOOD · NEW JERSEY

To My New Family

The Lairds

Acknowledgments

It was through the encouragement of my friends at the Revell Company that my first book, *That Girl in Your Mirror,* came into being and it was their confidence and interest that prompted the writing of this book. Along with the fine staff at Revell, I especially wish to thank Ruby Rhoades for her time and effort. I should also like to thank my husband, Andy, for his patience and for his assistance in the final preparation of the manuscript.

Preface

I knew when I became Miss America that it would be a year of terrific responsibility, but little did I dream that that responsibility would go on and on, long after my year as Miss America had ended and the crown had passed on to others. But it has— and in many ways I feel a deeper and more urgent responsibility than I ever felt during that plane-catching, glamor-filled whirlwind year.

During that year and since, as you young people began to know me, you've turned to me for answers to problems that you've found difficult to manage. I've talked personally to many of you and I've received thousands of letters from youth all across the country. You're having problems with Dad or Mom, or you wish you knew how to cope with a teacher who's giving you a difficult time. Many of you are being pressured or tempted to do things you're not sure you should. You are trying to find out who you are, what your life's purpose is, and where God fits into the busy world of America's teen-agers. Some of those letters I just didn't have time to answer adequately. Some of the personal interviews had to be cut short. So now I'm trying to answer many of the questions that you have asked me. I've changed the names, of course, and cut the letters to the essential questions.

Each letter represents some young person who has faith in my counsel and who is hopeful that I'll say something that will help solve his or her particular problem. I believe in telling you exactly what I feel, even though you may not agree with me or like what I have to say. You asked the question—I have to give my honest opinion.

I've said this before and I must say it again—I don't ever pretend to be an authority on personal problems. I'm not a psychologist and I'm not a trained counselor; I'm only just leaving *my* teens behind me. I speak from what I've experienced and observed and from what I believe to be right.

Another important thing I want to say—I write this book prayerfully. I firmly believe that each of us has been put in this world for a purpose—and God expects us to fulfill that purpose. He's shown me that at least a part of my reason for being here is to be as helpful as I can be to others and to witness His love and great power to work changes in human lives. Since that is my purpose, with His help, I hope to take every opportunity to carry it out.

For every one of you who has written me a letter, there are thousands more who have the same feelings, the same doubts and fears, hopes and dreams, but who haven't put them down on paper. It is for those unwritten letters, as well as the many I have received, that I write this book. I hope and pray that each of you will find in these pages some special message just for you —one that will help you work through your problems, gain self-confidence, and prepare for responsible adulthood.

Vonda Kay Van Dyke

Contents

DEAR VONDA KAY

1

My Problem Is Me . . .

"Some people never seem to have any problems. Why must I have so many?"

If you never had any problems, you'd be a very shallow and unsympathetic person, but I can't imagine any teen-ager *without* problems. Probably those who seem to have fewer have just learned to handle them better—and not to talk about them all the time.

You may as well recognize and admit your limitations and go on from that point. You must also recognize your potential and develop it. Everyone, without exception, has some special assets or talents just waiting to be used. So you need to know yourself and try to understand why you act and react the way you do.

You are bound to make mistakes, have successes and failures. You'll find some problems easier to solve than others and sometimes you'll need some outside help in figuring things out. The important thing is that you make progress, though it may be slow, toward becoming that person that you want to be.

Dear Vonda Kay,

Don't you think it's important to dress like everybody else? My mother says my skirts are too short, but everybody wears short skirts now. She wants me to pull my hair away from my face, but it's the style to let long hair fall down around your face. I think a girl should look and dress like other girls her age and not the way her mother did when she was a girl.

Lois

P.S. What do you think about mini-skirts? That would really make my mother mad.

Dear Lois,

Yes, I do think it's important to dress like "everybody else," but just take a look around you. Who is "everybody else"? There are so many kinds of people and so many different styles that you can't possibly be like them all. So I'm sure you must mean some special group in your school—and they must be very important to you.

No one likes to be different from the people he associates with most of the time, so I can imagine how you feel when your mother's tastes and your friends' tastes clash. Try pretending your friends are strangers to you and look them over carefully. Do they look really nice in the dresses and hair styles they are wearing—or does your mother have a point?

At a program the other day I sat next to a girl who was wearing a dress much more suitable for a tennis court than a stage performance. It was not at all attractive or appropriate. Before you raise your hemline, be sure that you can becomingly wear short skirts and that it's worth going to battle for.

As for hair style, I don't believe in saying "It's the style." For some girls, the long straight hair, if kept immaculately clean, is lovely. On others, it turns pretty girls into witches. Evaluate yourself—a mirror will help you out. Try pulling your hair away from your face. Experiment a bit. You might ask your mother's judgment. Maybe long hair is for you and you'll both recognize

16

the fact. If it isn't, don't worry about the other kids. Make yourself as attractive as possible.

About your P.S.—mini-skirts aren't for me.

Vonda Kay

Dear Vonda Kay,

I don't suppose a person like you, so beautiful and everything, could really understand how awful I feel. When you look at yourself you can be so proud and confident because you know you're pretty.

Sometimes I hate my looks. Nothing is right and no matter how nice my clothes are, I just plain look terrible. My hair is absolutely impossible, I'm short-waisted, I wear glasses and I have complexion troubles.

And please don't tell me the story of the ugly duckling—my mother is always doing that and it doesn't help. Besides, I'm fifteen and no change is taking place. How I envy you!

Susan

Dear Susan,

First of all, thank you for the compliment. I am remembering that back when I won the Miss America title, a former Miss America said to me, "Whenever you go to your mirror, just look in it and remember it is the same old you. No matter what people are saying to you and what wonderful things are said about you, you are still the same girl." So I try never to become proud or overconfident when nice things are said to me.

It shouldn't surprise you that I often find myself saying, when I look in the mirror, "I wish my hair were a bit prettier, and I could certainly use a little better nose. I really wouldn't mind having blue eyes—they are so attractive." So you see there are very few people who look at themselves in the mirror and are completely satisfied.

And even if they are beautiful on the outside, attractive to others and to themselves, that outside beauty is often marred by what is on the inside. Many beautiful girls are not happy with the way they've treated a friend or what they are doing with their lives or letting some opportunity slip by. They are not pleased with the way they face difficult situations. And at times, they aren't particularly happy with anything about their personalities.

I'm saying all this, Susan, to help you understand that no person is ever completely satisfied with himself or herself, as the case may be. Some of the prettiest girls are miserably unhappy about some fault they have.

Now—about you. You've spent a lot of time analyzing your faults. Okay, let's take a look at what you've found. "My hair is absolutely impossible!" You use a strong word there—absolutely—for this day and age. With all the wonderful modern helps for hair, you should be able to erase this from your list of faults. Go to a beauty salon and get your hair styled in a style that's right for your face and one that's easy to care for. Once you have it properly cut, you can take care of it yourself. If it's too curly, there are safe ways of straightening it. If it's straight, find a becoming style suited just to you and you're right in fashion, for most people want straight hair right now.

You can get around your short-waisted problems, too. A good saleswoman in a dependable dress shop or department store can help you find a dress shape and style that will completely camouflage your problem waist. From now on, be very careful in all your new clothes selections and soon your entire wardrobe will be exactly suited to you.

And glasses—what's wrong with that? You need them to see better, so accept that fact. They're part of you. Again, some good help in the choice of suitable frames for your own face is most important. I've seen many, many attractive people who must wear their glasses continually.

You also mention complexion troubles. Well, here's where the ugly-duckling story just could come true. So many teen-agers are bothered with this same problem. Have you seen a dermatologist about yours? They are specialists in this field and can often work wonders. Sometimes it does take time, but in the meantime

18

you can be meticulously clean, never let your face remain oily for long periods of time, drink lots of water, eat fruits and vegetables and avoid rich sweets and chocolate. The little duckling thought he was doomed for life, but he suddenly burst forth into something beautiful when the time was right.

You picked out your bad features—now try finding some good ones and be thankful for them. Even more, take a look at your personality. That is the most important and should be first on your "improvement list," for what you are inside will be reflected on the outside.

Vonda Kay

Dear Vonda Kay,

I think that the make-up emphasis that is being put on eyes these days is very flattering. My brother, who is older than I am and so I do sort of listen to him, thinks that girls look terrible when they use eyeliner. What do you think about it?

Nora

Dear Nora,

I'll have to agree with your brother that some girls look terrible wearing eyeliner. I have seen many high school girls wearing all sorts of eyeshadow, false eyelashes and mascara and, frankly, they look as if they're going to a costume party. This is probably what your brother is referring to.

There is a time and place for eyeliner. For high school girls, I think it should be used only for evenings and special occasions. It takes skill to use eyeliner properly and you should practice at home before you wear it in public.

I wear it most of the time, but I am careful not to choose stark black—that's too obvious. I like charcoal, brown, or a taupe shade, because they aren't so obvious, yet give the emphasis that eyes need.

One time I was being interviewed at a style show where several

19

older women were present. One of them remarked—and the others agreed—that it was refreshing to see a girl in my position who didn't wear eyeliner and all that sort of stuff. I said, "Thank you very much. You have given me a real compliment. Because, you see, I do wear it and the fact that you didn't realize it is a nice compliment."

So if you can wear it without being obvious, it may enhance your appearance. And, Nora, one other observation. I think you're lucky to have a brother a little older than you are and I'd suggest you pay attention to his opinion. Chances are that other fellows feel very much as he does.

Vonda Kay

Dear Vonda Kay,
    How can I go on a diet if my parents are against it? They say I'm still growing and need to eat. I am too heavy and I know it.

Lee

Dear Lee,
    Parents very early develop the need to see their babies gain weight. I've heard new mothers discussing their babies' weight gains and they get ecstatic over every ounce. And of course, those first months it is very important.

But somewhere along the years, parents should realize that a fat child is not necessarily a healthy child. Lots of girls feel they are too fat but their parents still insist they must eat.

On the other hand, some girls with very nice figures get the idea they're fat and want to try some radical diet. Their mothers do need to hold them back. Fad diets can be very dangerous to your health.

Since I don't know which you are, I'd suggest you get a height and weight chart. There's probably one in your health book at school. See how you measure up. A more convincing proof for both of you would be to see your family doctor. If you are overweight, let him prescribe a proper diet for you and ask your mother to help you follow it.

Vonda Kay

Dear Vonda Kay,

I tried out for a part in the junior class play. I really wanted it and thought I did well. Know what I'm doing? I'm in charge of make-up. How do you take a disappointment like that?

Jo

Dear Jo,

So you tried out for the junior class play and didn't make it? I wish I could tell you how many times this has happened to me. I ended up doing make-up one of those times, too, and I found it to be fascinating. It takes real skill to do a professional job and you'll find it's very exciting on the nights of the performances to be "where the action is."

I found reasons to be happy that I had that experience. I determined that I would do the best possible job and that I would learn something. I did—both.

If this is a field you are really interested in, then it is important that you learn all you can about it, both on stage and backstage, in the spotlight and out of it. Right now I'm a television major at UCLA. I don't especially want to run cameras all my life or set up lights—I'd rather be in front of the cameras—but I need to understand *everything* that goes into producing a show. I've learned to be grateful for learning experiences and to whole-heartedly support the cast and the director.

Good luck on the make-up. Be sure to take an old shirt of your Dad's to cover up your clothes—it's a messy job. And remember, there'll be a senior class play next year, and maybe you'll be the leading lady.

Vonda Kay

Dear Vonda Kay,

I don't know how to handle embarrassing situations—like not being able to answer a question in class or discovering that my slip has been showing all morning or singing something wrong in chorus or a million other things. I feel terrible for hours after I've done something like that.

Marlys

Dear Marlys,

A sense of humor is your surest defense. If you can laugh it off or make some joke about it, the situation is turned from an embarrassing one into a funny one. If you're not good with the quick quips, then just laugh, change the subject, and try to forget it ever happened.

Remember that you are probably the only one who ever gives such a situation a second thought. Everyone else has his own embarrassing moments to think about. So don't relive them and suffer them all over again by thinking about them.

Vonda Kay

Dear Vonda Kay,

Don't you ever get nervous when you appear in front of people? I can't even walk up to the front of the classroom without my legs getting stiff. Then I have to clear my throat and just keep clearing it. It's a terrible feeling and I wish I could die. Do you know of anything I can do to help myself?

Catherine

Dear Catherine,

I wonder if anyone ever gets completely over that "stage fright" feeling. Just about when I start thinking to myself that I don't get nervous any more—it happens again! Some especially difficult or uncomfortable situation arises and those old butterflies start to move around in my stomach. But it doesn't happen as much as it used to, and I think I know some of the reasons why. One reason might be that I accept these difficult situations as a tremendous challenge and I work very hard to conquer them.

I do appear before large crowds often and I'm sure that frequency helps one get over nervousness and that "freezing" feeling. Painful as it may sound to you, I'd advise you to get yourself in front of people as much as possible—volunteer to do an extra oral report, or to make a speech or to give the announcements in assembly.

You should know very thoroughly what you're going to say. Talk only about half as fast as you think you should, but about twice as loud. It's so easy to let your voice fade away. If people can't hear you or can't understand you because you talk too fast, they soon lose interest.

Something else I always tell myself is: These people are my friends. I am here because they asked me to share my thoughts and talents with them. Then I start talking just as I would with close friends and—I soon forget I'm in front of people.

Try it out. It's amazing but those "stiff" legs of yours will move and you'll get through it. Then—you've done it once, you can do it again.

Vonda Kay

Dear Vonda Kay,

How do you keep such a good figure? So many of my friends are starting to get fat and we are all self-conscious about it. If you diet, what diet do you follow?

Erica

Dear Erica,

The best way to keep a nice figure is to watch what you eat and discipline yourself at the table. I know many young people live on French fries, hamburgers and soft drinks as a steady diet. You can't expect to lose weight or to keep a nice figure on that.

I'm fortunate to be married to a man who believes diet—not dieting—is very important. We try to eat things that are good for us physically, and don't eat just for enjoyment or entertainment.

I eat a lot of vegetables, fresh and cooked, meat, and fresh fruits. I try to avoid sweets and starches—no bread or potatoes. For me, this is successful. Others may have a more serious weight problem and should see their family doctor.

Surely, at your age, you girls can do it by just saying, "No, thank you." Get in the habit early in life and you won't have lots of pounds to take off the hard way later. The person who said the best way to lose weight is to push yourself away from the table was so right.

Vonda Kay

Dear Vonda Kay,

I have a terrible temper and I know it. When things go against me, or I can't decide what to wear, or someone is using the phone and I want it, or a dozen other things—I'll stomp up the stairs or slam doors or yell at someone. Ordinarily I'm quite likeable, I think, but frustration and anger really set me off. Am I hopeless?

Cindy

Dear Cindy,

I once read a little book which suggested that a person could be nearly perfect in all areas of personality except for one—and that one, temper, could completely erase all the other good qualities he possessed.

24

Though you are a sweet and dear person with many wonderful qualities, when you lose your temper, Cindy, you're considered childish, immature and lacking in discipline and self-control. And somehow that is what people remember about you.

Anger is something you have to learn to control, and I have read that some people have more temper to control every fifteen minutes than others may have in a whole day. You may be one of those who have more to do, and that means you must work at it harder than ever.

I guess that anger is a two-part experience. First you have feelings of frustration, resentment or whatever it is, and then comes your response to it. The latter is the easier one for which to find methods of control. Devise some ways to handle yourself when you feel that top ready to blow. Maybe a good friend, or a member of your family, could suggest, "Hold it, Cindy, let's count slowly to 25," or, "Let's run around the block or take a bike ride"—anything to keep you from saying things in anger that you'll always regret.

The first part, controlling those feelings that cause the outbursts, is something you can't do alone, and you may as well admit it. Some things we just don't seem to have the strength to conquer on our own, but must seek outside help. Make this a matter of daily personal prayer. The best "outside help" comes through Jesus Christ and you can be assured that if you seek it, you shall find it.

Vonda Kay

Dear Vonda Kay,
  How do you overcome shyness? How can a shy girl talk to a shy boy?

Karin

Dear Karin,
  Probably the shy boy is wondering the same thing, and with just a little encouragement. . . .

25

Everybody can smile. Try that for a beginning. Not many people can resist a smile. It's almost automatic to smile when someone smiles at you.

After a couple of times of just smiling, add a "Hi." It doesn't have to be a big production, just a natural and friendly "Hi."

You can't just suddenly say to yourself, "I'm no longer shy." But as you work at it, bit by bit, you will find that each attempt is easier than the one before. Be interested in other people, listen to them when they talk and try to comment on the things they say. The first time it may seem very difficult and you'll have to force yourself, but if you do it once, you'll find you can again, and pretty soon it will become easy for you.

Vonda Kay

Dear Vonda Kay,

My hair gets oily almost right after I wash it. Is it all right to wash hair every other day or so, or is that hard on it? Someone told me that would destroy all the natural oil.

Betty Lou

Dear Betty Lou,

Many people have the same problem of oily hair that you do. It does not damage hair to wash it often, every other day if you need it. Maybe in the summer you'll require a daily shampoo. This way your hair will always look shiny and soft. Do get a good natural bristle hairbrush and use the 100-stroke-a-day treatment. A cream rinse and hair conditioner might be beneficial, too. I'm not going to give you a commercial on my favorite brands, but I would suggest that you talk with a beautician about those that are best for you. Just one appointment and you'll have the professional advice to help you for a long time.

Vonda Kay

Dear Vonda Kay,

My memory seems to play tricks on me at some of the most important times. I'll be introducing two of my friends and I really know them both well. You can guess what happens. I'll forget one of the names. I can't seem to help it and feel so sorry when I do it. What can I do to smooth it over?

Pat

Dear Pat,

This is indeed an awkward situation. I feel sorry for those who have a hard time remembering names, or who just seem to "blank out" on introductions, because it happens to me now and then.

If it happens only rarely, just simply say, "I'm sorry, but I've forgotten your name." Then as quickly as possible you might say something about the person, indicating that you really do know him—"He's on the tennis team at Central High" or some such comment to help place him and to pass over your own slip.

If you have a lapse in memory often at introduction time, you might devise some clever way to get through it which you can resort to every time it happens. For instance, "I really want you two to meet but I have a terrible time with middle names." Or, "If I were sure my memory wouldn't blank out, I'd introduce you two." Friends will take the cue and say their own names.

A sense of humor is a precious gift. If you are so blessed, you are fortunate because it will help you so often. If you are not, you can at least laugh (outwardly) at yourself, which is better than stammering and turning red.

Vonda Kay

Dear Vonda Kay,

I have a reputation for always being late. Everybody teases me about it, but sometimes my family or friends get mad. I al-

ways think I give myself enough time, but I never seem to make it. Could you suggest something to help me?

Trudy

Dear Trudy,

You have my sympathy, because I once had a reputation for always being late. A very dear lady who has done a great deal for me in helping prepare for the Miss America Pageant and in just being a friend taught me something about promptness. In her sweet way, she said to me, "Honey, you are a wonderful person and you know I consider you almost perfect. Now, I know you won't be late for our shopping appointment tomorrow."

I think she was saying something else to me, more like "Honey, this is one habit you are going to have to break. I expect you to be there on time and if you respect me, you'll do it."

Now when I see the clock ticking away, nearer and nearer an appointed hour, I still remember her and push full steam ahead.

If you have respect for other people, you won't keep them waiting. If you have pride in yourself, you will come through as you promised you would.

How you do it is up to you. Set your clock ahead, start a half hour earlier, work toward an earlier goal—you must discover your own way. But do it right away. Your friends and family should be able to take you at your word.

Vonda Kay

Dear Vonda Kay,

I'm so tired of everybody's saying, "Be yourself." I don't seem to know who I am and so I can't find much help in being told to just be "me." It seems to me that may be all right for a girl who is pretty and popular and satisfied with herself. But for one who is self-conscious and confused, it just doesn't help. Do you have any answers to this business of knowing who you are?

Rosemary

Dear Rosemary,

There is a lot of talk these days about identity and self-discovery. That seems to be what is troubling you, just as it does so many teens. You know, it really isn't a new problem. People have asked the question for centuries. Many of the great philosophers suggested that one of life's most important questions is—who are we, who am I? Am I soul, personality, intellect, or what? No one really has a definite answer or the question wouldn't keep coming back.

Even the girl who is pretty and self-assured should never be satisfied with herself. There is always room for improvement, and everyone should continually set goals toward which to work for self-betterment.

You suggest you feel self-conscious. That doesn't make you different from others. Probably even the President of the United States feels that way sometimes. And I know that entertainers, even the professionals, do. So don't be discouraged, friend.

I have often told girls, "Be yourself," and when I do, I mean several things. First of all, you must have self-respect. I don't even know you, Rosemary, but I do know that you have some special quality or talent, or more than one. Everybody does—without exception. I suspect that you have spent too much time tearing yourself down. Look on the positive side. What are your good qualities? Are you a good student? Athletic? Musical talent? Good with children? Nice personality? Dependable? Pick out all the good traits you can think of and don't ever forget them! These should give you some self-confidence and help you to like that person called *yourself*.

Secondly, let's face it—the real you is made of many "you's." The person you most admire, the glamorous, popular girl of your daydreams, the heroine of the book you're reading, your favorite teacher, your best friend and maybe even your worst enemy. Each day you find yourself trying on certain qualities that you admire in that person. But be careful as you experiment. Don't go to extremes that don't fit you or that make you uncomfortable. For instance, a very capable, organized girl can't suddenly play the helpless baby-doll type. But she can dig into some committee and really produce—and make friends along the way. Some girls just aren't as coordinated for gymnastics as others. I've seen a girl friend work for hours trying to turn a perfect cartwheel and never make it. But that same girl had a knack for painting stage scenery that put her in demand for every play our school produced.

Third, I haven't yet met a person who doesn't have a smile. To be sure, some people don't use theirs very much, but everyone has one. Don't hide yours! That's one of the most personal things about any person—his or her very own smile. To be yourself— use yours!

Know yourself—your strengths and weaknesses. That's who you really are even if you're trying your wings at being someone different. Try to relax when you're with people, either those of your own age or others much older. Be sincere in what you say and do. Folks will like you best that way and the more others like you, the more you'll like yourself.

You are a very special person, Rosemary, so smile about it!

Vonda Kay

Dear Vonda Kay,

The girl who was chosen Valentine Queen at our school wasn't really pretty at all. Her legs are heavy and she just isn't that good-looking. Some of the rest of us who ran against her got to wondering about such elections. Doesn't a school want a really pretty girl to represent it?

Lauren

Dear Lauren,

Have you ever watched a Miss America beauty pageant on TV? If you're like most people, as you watch the lovely girls parade across your TV screen you choose someone you think should get the crown. How often have you selected the one who was ultimately named the winner? Many of those who appear to be the most beautiful never make the top five, or even the top ten.

Most contests, fortunately, are not judged on the physical features alone. Many times the really terrific looking girl does not come out on top—it's the attractive gal with the terrific personality who walks off with the honors. You see, it isn't physical features alone that make a person beautiful, it's a vibrant, friendly personality.

If your school wants a pretty girl to represent it, my guess is that they chose one. Evidently the majority of the kids do think she is pretty and if I were you, I'd take a second look at her and find out why. The rest of you may think you're prettier, but she's obviously got something you don't have and you'd be wise to discover what it is.

If you're a pretty girl physically, you're very fortunate, and you should work hard on making your personality match your looks—you'll be a sure winner someday! One of the first things you'd better work on is to take losing more gracefully than you have done. Instead of tearing the winner apart, take a look at yourself.

Beauty is so much more than just what meets the eye. You are discovering that fact in high school; I saw it there, in my college, in the Miss State contest and the Miss America Pageant. I travel now, performing and emceeing for many state and local beauty pageants which are preliminaries to the Miss America Pageant. I know what I'm talking about, Lauren, because I see it every day.

I also see hundreds of losers and the kind I like best are those who can sincerely go to the winner, give her a hug and say she deserved it. They may shed some tears later in their rooms, but they don't get catty and critical about the girl who beat them out.

Vonda Kay

P.S. Just recently I met a young girl who possessed *every* quality of a winner. I saw her at a state pageant. She was pretty, but more important, she was very sweet, sincere and friendly.

I learned just before the top ten were announced that, although she had been a runner-up the year before, she had not made the top ten this year. I watched her face steadily as they made the announcements. A woman near me, active in stage production, said, "My, what a shame. Someone had better be with her after they leave the stage. What will she do?" The woman's superior simply said, "No, she'll not need anyone. She's so poised and such a beautiful person inside that she'll be a gracious loser— even though this means a great deal to her."

As the names were read, she simply stood a little straighter and kept her pretty smile. What deeper compliment could she have been given? People watch even a loser and sometimes gain more from the way she handles her loss than they do from the winner and her triumph.

2

That Family of Mine

My mother. . . . My sister. . . . Why does my dad . . . ?
Even grandmother. . . . Family living brings all kinds of problems. Maybe the house is too small, little sister a nuisance or
mother "just doesn't understand."

Some situations can't be changed and the family you're given
is one of them. So it's up to you to accept and adjust to that
problem as it is.

In a way, your family is a little world in itself, and your ability
to get along there will probably be reflected in your ability to
get along in the larger world outside of your home. There are,
and always will be, rules and regulations, and you may as well
learn to live with them.

Remember, too, that everyone in your family is constantly
changing, just as you are. You have to learn some flexibility to
make the necessary adjustments. So go to work on yourself, and
be grateful for the love and good times you share with your
family.

Dear Vonda Kay,

My mother is a stickler on hours—I have to be in at ten o'clock on week nights and eleven on weekends. What can anyone do and get home at that time? The movies aren't out till eleven and if you want a soda or hamburger—forget it! I can't go out with boys because they don't know what to do on such an early date. Maybe those hours were what my mother had to observe, but they're not practical today. If you'd just say something, she'd listen, because she's always talking about—"Now, a girl like Vonda Kay Van Dyke. . . ." So, please. . . .

Carrie

Dear Carrie,

I get the feeling that you're putting me on the spot, trying to prove something to your mother. Well, I'll be honest. That ten o'clock curfew on week nights doesn't really sound too bad. That was the dorm hour my first year at college. During the week you need time for study and you should get adequate rest, too.

My parents set a weekend curfew of 11:30 for me when I was in high school. Of course, I thought it was too early and very inconvenient at times, but I did find it was possible to take in an earlier movie and still have time for a hamburger and coke. Since this was the hour my parents had set, I observed it. I respected my parents' wishes and I wanted to show them I was responsible. If something did come up and we saw we weren't going to make it, I'd always find a phone and call them.

Many parents can't get to sleep until their children are in and they know that everything is all right, so you are making it hard for them by staying out late. When they make a rule, it is up to you to observe it. Maybe if you show you are responsible and cooperative, you just might be able to get your mother to stretch it to 11:30—that extra half-hour does relieve the rush and gives time to enjoy the last bite of hamburger.

Vonda Kay

34

Dear Vonda Kay,

I think that my room should be the one place where I have privacy. My mother is always going in when I'm not there and putting things away, snooping into my pocketbook and notebooks when she does it. She pretends she's cleaning up my room, which I must admit is a wreck. But it is my room—I want a place of my own where no one is nosing around. Is that asking too much?

Kim

Dear Kim,

Of course you want privacy—and you have an easy way to get it. You keep your room as neat as your mother keeps the rest of the house and she'll have no reason to be in it all the time. You've asked for her presence by letting things get in such a mess. Hang up your clothes, put your books away, keep things in order—and you'll have your privacy.

I can't help wondering, though, Kim, what it is that you don't want your mother to find. If she is in your room because she suspects that you are hiding something from her, then no amount of cleaning is going to help. All I can say is that—more than just your room—you had better keep your life in order, too.

Vonda Kay

Dear Vonda Kay,

Some of my friends' mothers are so pretty and young looking. My mother always looks sloppy even when she's supposed to be dressed up. She's fat and bulgy and her hair is always frizzy. She's my mother and I love her because she's good to me and everything. But when she comes to school for something, I try to avoid her because I'm ashamed. She's an officer or something in the P.T.A. and lots of people see her. Even the teachers know her and they must think she's an awful slob. I can't go on acting as if I don't know her, but . . .

Fran

Dear Fran,

Act as if you don't know her? Now isn't that a little childish? I'd suggest you take a second, deeper look at this woman who is your mother. She must have some very fine qualities that put her in places of leadership and win the respect of teachers and administrators. You should be very proud. She's good to you and you love her. And I just bet a lot of other people do, too, because it is not the outward appearance alone that makes a person lovable, it is something inside. Like a shabby house—if there is love and happiness inside, it becomes a home. Somehow, just from what you say, I feel I'd like to know your mother.

Still, I think you could be helpful to her if you would do it kindly. For example, if you see a nice hair style in a magazine, you might say, "Hey, Mom, I bet this would look great on you!" Either you try fixing it for her or get her to suggest it to the beautician.

Go shopping with her and suggest things that look well on her. Maybe if she complains about her own "bulges" you could suggest she get a new, different type of girdle, or volunteer to go on a diet with her. Don't be rude, but act in love. She may be so flattered by your awareness of her as a person that she'll look to you for advice and take your suggestions.

Most of all, remember that you do love her and let that show in everything you do.

Vonda Kay

Dear Vonda Kay,

How much work do you think a girl should be expected to do around the house? My mother seems to think I'm a servant or something the way she lays out the jobs. None of my friends have to do as much as I do.

Alice

Dear Alice,

All through grade school and high school I was responsible for certain household chores—dishes, vacuuming, and so on. These tasks were expected of me and for them I got a weekly allowance. I'm sure the allowance was some motivation, although it wasn't large. I even cooked dinner three or four nights of the week. Some of my girl friends, like yours, didn't have to help around the house. Now they are married and have discovered there are so many things they don't know how to do—like fix their husbands a complete and delicious dinner. I am very thankful, and so is my husband, that I had such preparation.

So, pick up that broom—and learn all you can about housekeeping. Someday you'll need it.

Vonda Kay

Dear Vonda Kay,

Some of my girl friends and I like to go walking together, on Saturday afternoon or in the evening. We go to the Dari-Queen for ice cream or just walk around. Naturally we run into boys lots of times and then stand around the street and talk. Or just walk together and have lots of fun. My mother thinks I'm chasing the boys when I do this and we always fight about it. She says it's cheap. We're not doing anything bad at all. I don't understand why she makes such a fuss.

Maria

Dear Maria,

Really, I don't think your mother is being unreasonable at all. She has a legitimate reason for asking you not to walk the streets, especially at night. If you'd be honest about it, you *do* do it to meet boys, don't you? Maybe the particular ones you meet now are all right, but usually the guys who pick up girls on the street aren't the most desirable. Can't your group of girls take turns getting together at different houses? The boys will soon get the idea and come around and then your mother can know what kind of fellows they are. Just sit on the steps and talk or listen to records. You can still have a good time but in a much safer, more respectable way.

Your mother is just thinking of your reputation and your safety and I think you should abide by what she says.

Vonda Kay

Dear Vonda Kay,

I have a little sister who drives me crazy. She's seven and I'm fifteen. Whenever my friends come over, she has to start showing off and being a real brat. We can't talk or listen to records or anything because she starts singing real loud or saying, "Look at me."

She also gets into my drawers and shows my things to her friends when I'm not around. The more I ask her to leave my things alone or to get out of the room when my friends are there, the more stubborn she gets. If I hit her, she goes bawling to my mother and I get it. There must be some way to get rid of her but I haven't found it.

Lynn

Dear Lynn,

Can't you see that your little sister is really saying she admires you very much? True, it's an odd way to do it, but that's why she wants to show her friends your things and brag about her "big sister." Little girls can have some very obnoxious ways of trying to be accepted. So she drives you crazy, and I bet you both drive your mother crazy.

Next time you bring your friends home, turn the tables on her. Suggest that she sing for your friends before you put the records on—and ask your friends to listen to her for just a little while. You might even clue them in before they come into your house. Then thank her very sincerely and tell her you want to listen to records now. If she has had your undivided attention for a little while, she will very likely leave willingly.

Or talk it over with your mother, but not when your sister is crying because you hit her nor when you're upset. Do it at a time when there is no tension so you can both think more clearly. Maybe she can suggest errands for your sister during the time you entertain friends.

Even if she does get in your hair, there's an awful lot to be learned about life through family living—sharing, respecting the rights of others, learning to work out problems. Be honest now —you'd miss that little sister dreadfully if she weren't around, wouldn't you? Let her know it and see if it changes things.

Vonda Kay

Dear Vonda Kay,

Up to now my mother and I have gotten along real well together. My friends liked her when I brought them home. But since I've been in high school, things have seemed to change and now I'm embarrassed to bring friends, either boys or girls, home.

She so wants to be a part of things that she tries to make like one of the kids. She jokes with the boys and she gossips with my girl friends about other girls. We do it, too, but coming from her it sounds different and makes us all uncomfortable.

Her feelings get hurt easily and I don't want to hurt her, but I'm getting so ashamed I don't want to bring friends home any more.

Can you help?

Laura

Dear Laura,

This is an interesting switch. Usually it's the mother who sees her daughter developing undesirable traits of hers. Here you are seeing your mother reflect a bad habit of yours. If she is gossiping, where does she get the gossip to repeat? Undoubtedly it came from you. When you do it, it doesn't seem so bad, but when you hear it from someone else, it sounds terrible. In my book, *That Girl in Your Mirror,* I said that manners are like new shoes; you wear them around the house to break them in before you wear them outside. I believe it is very, very important to have good manners at home, and gossiping is not good manners.

One of the women I have most admired in my entire lifetime and who was very instrumental in helping me start into the Miss America Pageants is a lovely lady. She was extremely helpful to me during my reign as Miss Arizona and always acted in good taste in every kind of situation. But the thing I remember most about her is that I *never* heard her say an ungracious word about anyone. This is a trait we should all learn and if you demonstrate it at home, I bet your mother will follow your example.

Maybe, too, for some reason she missed out on youthful fun and she's sort of reliving her youth through you and your friends. I would make a guess that it is more annoying to you than to your friends. Accept her and be thankful she takes an interest in you—some girls wish their mothers would.

Vonda Kay

Dear Vonda Kay,

How can I tell my Dad, without hurting his feelings, that I'm growing up? He seems to think I'm still a little girl and comes into my room anytime, even the bathroom. Sometimes I want some privacy, and I want him to know that at fourteen a girl is growing up. What should I do? Otherwise, I get along real well with him.

Libby

Dear Libby,

Sometimes it's hard for fathers to realize their dear little girls are turning into young ladies and have need of some privacy. They may know it in their hearts but don't want to admit it, just

40

because they don't quite know how to treat you as a grown-up girl. Ask your mother to help you out. Or take it on yourself and gently remind him when he comes into your room, "Hey, Dad, how about a little warning knock? I am a young lady, you know." It won't take him long to get the point.

Vonda Kay

Dear Vonda Kay,
   The telephone seems to be the reason for lots of disagreement at our house. Surely it's there to be used, so why all the noise when I talk to my friends for awhile?

Sally

Dear Sally,
   A telephone serves several purposes. It should be available for incoming calls as well as in use for friendly conversations. Even if it's not being used, it is serving a purpose.
   I think you should limit the length of your conversations. In my early high school days, I was limited to ten minutes per phone call per night. I didn't necessarily like it, but I do think it was conducive to good conversations and cut down on long, gossipy calls. It also gave me more study time. Don't be unreasonable when your folks limit you. That call that's trying to get in just might be the one you've been hoping for all week.

Vonda Kay

Dear Vonda Kay,
   This may be a hard question for you to help me with, because I understand that you are an only child. But you've talked to others and maybe you can offer something to help me out.
   I have a sister who's just a year and a half younger than I. She's everything that I wish I were. So outgoing and friendly. She's prettier than I am and attracts the fellows, when I can hardly get a second look. She's the one of the two of us that

41

people always remember. We get along just fine most of the time and she's really sweet to me, but I just can't seem to conquer my jealousy. Sometimes I almost hate her and then I feel guilty about it because she can't really help it. It's got to be my fault— but what can I do?

Judy

Dear Judy,

You do have a problem, don't you? Usually we have to deal with unpleasant qualities in other people, and here you are discovering those qualities in yourself and finding only the fine things in your sister. It's always easier if the fault lies in the other person.

No, I've never had a sister and I can only imagine what that relationship is, but I have met many people in life whom I've admired for different abilities or traits that they possessed and that I didn't. Some were very close girl friends in school. Jealousy would creep in sometimes, but I would always try to figure out what that person had that made him or her so attractive to other people. Then I'd take a look at myself and try to find ways of developing those same traits in my life.

To prove a point I want to make—try something for me. Take a look at yourself in your mirror and then walk away. Try to picture your face as you saw it. It's hard, isn't it? Or think of some one of your friends, maybe one you've just met or even someone you've known for years. Try to make a picture in your mind of that person's face, exactly as he or she looks. Don't you find your memory is a little short on all the details of facial features, hair, etc.? So you begin to remember his or her personality instead, because that can't be separated from outside features.

You say your sister is the one that people always remember. Don't you see it's not necessarily because she's prettier, even though she may be—but more likely because of her personality? She's shown them kindness; she's shown them friendliness. She's given something of herself to each one. And that's something every one of us can do—give of ourselves. You may not be able

42

to change your looks, but you can add a smile and cheery greeting. You can stand by to listen to someone's troubles or offer a helping hand when it's needed.

You know something else? It's just very possible that your sister admires something in you very much, too. And if she's conquered the envy part, she is free to work on being like that which she admires.

I think that another thing you can do is refer to the Scriptures. I rather like the Living Letters version of the Scriptures as it talks about love. "Love is never envious," it says. You love your sister, but love is not envious. So be proud of her, always build her up and seek to incorporate her good qualities into your own life—and be sure to give of yourself to other people.

Vonda Kay

Dear Vonda Kay,
My mother and dad have some pretty bad times together. They fight about such crazy little things and then won't talk to each other for ages. They really get mad and yell and say mean things. It makes me want to hide somewhere. Sometimes I walk out of the house and think I'll never go back, but of course I always do. Maybe they should get a divorce. I guess that's pretty bad, too, but I don't see how they can stand much more of this —I sure can't.

Tommy

Dear Tommy,
Having grown up in a loving atmosphere, I can only imagine how upsetting your parents' situation is for you. If they knew what it is doing to you, they might try harder to get along. However, it is not up to you to say which is right for them—divorce or the way they are now living. They will have to make their own decision on that.

But you should try very hard not to take sides. Don't let either one of them use things you may say against the other. Try to show them that you love them both. They must be dreadfully miserable, too, and in need of love. Pray always that God's love will conquer their human hatred and weakness and become an important bond within your family.

Vonda Kay

Dear Vonda Kay,

My brother is almost two years older than I am. He's always been my parents' favorite child and gets away with all kinds of things that I wouldn't even dare try. When he talks at the table, they listen to every word and ask questions and laugh with him. If I start to tell something that happened, they usually interrupt me and talk about something else—with him. If I do finish a story, they just say absent-minded like, "Yeah, wasn't that nice?" and go on to something else. Gee, sometimes I think I could just disappear and they wouldn't even notice. I'm tired of being a nobody at our house and I don't think that parents should have favorites among their children.

Caroline

Dear Caroline,

I really doubt if your parents are playing favorites, though I can understand why it seems so to you. You and your brother are two different people and you draw out different responses from your parents.

Perhaps your brother talks about things that are of much more interest to adults than you do. Next time, listen very carefully and try to discover why he appears to be more interesting than you are. Then analyze the things you tell them about.

Do you talk about yourself all the time? That can become awfully boring to others. Do you make fun of others, dispute things they say or complain about everything? No one enjoys that kind of conversation. Try listening to the others and asking them questions about the things they're discussing. If your parents have gone some place during the day, ask them about it. You might find something out about your Dad's job. Be interested in them and I can just bet they'll respond and start taking an interest in the things you have to say.

Vonda Kay

Dear Vonda Kay,

My grandmother lives with us and sometimes I almost hate her. She sticks her nose in everything. Whenever I ask my folks for something, she has to express her opinion and boy, is she old-fashioned. I know they listen to her, too. Once I yelled at her and she started crying and my mother made me go to my room and it was a mess. She's very healthy so it looks like I'll have the problem a long time. I'm only fourteen and not going out with boys, but I hate to think what it's going to be like then. She'll probably sit in the living room every time I have someone in. It's really an impossible set-up.

Doris

Dear Doris,

I hope your mother didn't see the letter you wrote to me. You do have a real problem and I'm sympathetic, but your lack of respect for older people isn't a very pretty thing to see and surely must be upsetting to your mother. Someday she may need to live with you; would you want your daughter to speak of her as you just have of her mother?

It is an uncomfortable and far from ideal situation to have three generations in one home. Sometimes it's necessary, though, and at such times everyone needs to learn to make the best of it. Do you suppose it's easy for your mother to have someone always "helping" her but wanting to do it some other way?

When you want to discuss something important, I'd suggest that you ask your parents to come to your room, or speak to them when your grandmother is resting.

When the time comes for you to entertain friends, perhaps your family could fix up the recreation room or panel a room in the basement that could be yours. It should be made clear that the room is yours. I can imagine your grandmother would be just as glad not to be around for your records, conversation and jokes.

You can't imagine, Doris, how often young people write me about their "old-fashioned" parents. You're lucky if you get along with them and find only your grandmother old-fashioned.

This is one of those situations that you can't change but must adjust yourself to. You can go through it filled with resentment and hatred and making life difficult for everybody. Or you can make an effort to adjust and find ways to work out each problem as it arises.

Please try to be patient; even show your grandmother some extra little kindness. Sometimes life isn't too pleasant for elderly people—they need love and attention just as you do. If you work at it a little, she just might turn out to be a good friend.

Vonda Kay

3

Outside of My Family—
Friends, Teachers . . .

Getting along with others can be very trying. Some people seem to have all the friends they could possibly want, and others can't seem to make or keep any. And in between are the troubles that come in trying to understand the friends you do have.

It's good to know and like many different people. This will help you grow in your interests and ability to get along with others. Being a member of an exclusive clique can close the door to some wonderful growing experiences in friendship.

Of course you'll have problems with your friends. No one is perfect. They're probably having them with you, too. The ability to get along with people doesn't just happen; it's something you have to work at.

In order to make new friends you must be friendly. Be interested in other people and their joys and problems. Be an enthusiastic person; enjoy a coke at the local diner as much as a full course dinner at some elite restaurant.

To have good friends, you must be one.

Dear Vonda Kay,

There's a new girl who just came to our school. I'd like to be friendly but once before I was first to make friends with a new girl and she turned out to be a real pain. I thought I'd never get away from her. How can I find out what this girl is like without having her hang onto me all the time?

Mariann

Dear Mariann,

One unfortunate experience doesn't mean that all similar ones are going to turn out the same way. Treat each new person you meet as a distinct individual and don't prejudge anyone from past experience. You might miss out on a wonderful friendship.

A cheery smile will do wonders to encourage someone new. If you've ever had to face a whole school of new faces, you'll understand. The stranger wants to be accepted, so if she seems to cling to the first person who befriends her, try to sympathize. Introduce her to other girls so she makes several friends at once. That will give you both the time and opportunity to know each other. This girl just might turn out to be one of your best friends.

Vonda Kay

Dear Vonda Kay,

I have several really good friends, seven of us to be exact, and we've been close for several years. Lately we've been fighting a lot and we get mad when one or two go someplace together and the whole group doesn't go. We like each other a great deal, but what makes us act this way and what can we do about it?

Laura

Dear Laura,

A clique can become a very powerful force in your life. It controls what you wear, where you go and how you act. Yet most every girl strives to work her way into one group or another.

When I was in junior high there was a rather exclusive group of us that went everywhere together. I had to work my way into it because I wasn't accepted right away. That process alone can use a lot of time and nervous energy and cause a great deal of frustration. But I made it and the eight of us were a tight little group of our own. After reaching my goal, I really had my doubts as to its significance.

Fortunately, when we went into high school the group sort of dissolved and instead of having seven girl friends, I had a best friend or two and then found friends in many different groups. This takes off the pressure of conforming and eliminates the competition and jealousy that often exist in a clique.

It would seem that maybe you girls need a change. Perhaps you've gotten too close to each other and it's a source of friction. Your interests may be changing from what they were when you first got together and you find you're not so compatible. I'd suggest you either open up your ranks and get new faces and ideas in your group, or that each of you individually start reaching out and finding new friends.

This probably would have to be a group decision and maybe your friends don't feel about it as you do. That means you will have to act on your own and perhaps face the hostility of the others.

I do think every girl needs a "best friend" and I hope you always have one. There are so many little events and feelings that you want to confide and you need someone who will understand, share her feelings with you and be able to keep confidence.

Vonda Kay

Dear Vonda Kay,

I have a girl friend with a bad reputation. Everyone keeps telling me I'll get the same kind of name, even though my own morals are of the highest. I do care what people say. Should I try to get rid of her, and how can I do it gracefully?

Nelda

Dear Nelda,

Reputations are such tricky things and yet so terribly important. Sometimes they really fit the person's conduct and other times they are very unjust. If you know that your friend merits the bad name she has gotten, then you are in a touchy spot. If you are seen with her a lot, it just naturally seems to be assumed that you are like her, high morals or no. Then you should probably see less of her and not go places with her alone, but try to include her in a group of girls. Do keep in contact with her because you may be able to help her get back on the right track again.

Perhaps, though, she is being judged unjustly from some rumor that has gotten started, or for some other reason. It would seem wrong to end your friendship and leave her out in the cold. Standing by a friend in trouble is a mark of loyalty. Why don't you try enlarging your circle of friends? Explain to a few of them what happened so they will accept her. It's a serious and heartbreaking situation to be accused of something you are not guilty of.

Vonda Kay

Dear Vonda Kay,

One of my friends is very loud. Every time I go someplace with her she always embarrasses me and every time I meet a boy she always ruins it by telling him everything she can about me. I've tried to stay away from her but our mothers are friends and

50

you know how that is. How should I tell her to stop it and not hurt her feelings?

Sandy

Dear Sandy,

Sometimes in life we have to run the risk of hurting someone's feelings in order to get some problem worked out. Since you are somewhat obligated to keep this friendship, you need to work it out and the only way to do that is to talk it out. Do it as nicely as you possibly can, explaining that it embarrasses you and makes things difficult for you. And you should take care that she doesn't have questionable things to report about you.

Vonda Kay

Dear Vonda Kay,

I'm a member of the Girl Scouts but I can't stand going because I always get left out of things. I've talked to my leader about this but she just tells me to be friendly. I've tried but they still ignore me. How can I stop being left out?

Claudia

Dear Claudia,

One of the best places to get experience in getting along with others is in the Girl Scouts. I have happy memories of my Scouting years and think it's a beneficial experience for any girl. So I hope you stick with it.

Your leader is right in saying you should be friendly. Being friendly is more than just saying hello and smiling. You have to give of yourself, too. Take part in the activities. Maybe do KP now and then when you don't really have to. Help make the plans for special activities so you can be working in smaller groups and really get to know other girls better.

51

It's a lonely feeling to be left out and I sincerely hope you can soon remedy the situation.

Vonda Kay

Dear Vonda Kay,

Some of the girls in my class (ninth grade) are forming sort of a club and inviting others to join. They call it a sorority. I've been asked but my mother questions the whole deal since it's going to leave some girls out and she says they'll be hurt. Couldn't they form their own or something? And should I not join and then be hurt, too, just because of them?

Sandi

Dear Sandi,

Your mother has very good reasons for questioning such a group. It can lead into serious problems and be a source of unhappiness for the girls who are left out. Any such group that is not sanctioned by the school and has no adult leadership or control is a dangerous one.

If you really think you have something, why don't you talk to the principal or activities advisor? Maybe the school would sponsor it and a faculty member could be assigned to it.

If your friends turn up their noses at such a suggestion, then it's probably because they want to be very exclusive and I'd say you'd better not put your name on the membership roll.

Vonda Kay

Dear Vonda Kay,

What would you do if your best girl friend also liked your boy friend and always came between the two of you?

Candy

Dear Candy,

It's hard for me to understand how a really "best" girl friend could keep hurting your friendship with your boy friend. That's not being much of a friend and it certainly makes an uncomfortable situation for all three.

I think it's time to make some changes—either a new girl friend or a new boy friend. And you're the only one who can say which of the two is more important to you.

Vonda Kay

Dear Vonda Kay,

I have a teacher that just plain makes fun of kids. She thinks it's teasing, but it's really just mean. Like braces or something we wear, or boy friends and girl friends, or even our names, or the way we walk. It's awful. We wouldn't dare complain or she'd make a joke of us in front of the class.

Can you think of something we can do?

Beth

Dear Beth,

I have always found it difficult to understand how one person can deliberately hurt or be cruel to another. Yet mocking and taunting others seems to go on a lot among teen-agers today. I wonder if maybe your teacher is trying to be a part of your activities and to be accepted by you. This is what she sees and hears you do, so she tries to join in on your way of treating each other—to be like you and liked by you.

But, whatever her reasons, they have obviously gone too far since you and your friends are embarrassed and hurt. I believe you should go directly to her and seriously explain that some of you are very ill at ease in her class. Tell her that she does often embarrass you and hurt your feelings. She may not even realize it, you know.

I hope you'll give it a try. I think your very honesty about it and your confidence in talking with her will show her she's accepted. Then she won't need to try so hard, nor will she make fun of you for having called it to her attention.

Vonda Kay

Dear Vonda Kay,

My mother has called my attention to something my friends and I tend to do that is very discourteous. We barge into each other's houses in groups and never even speak to the girl's parents. Or maybe one of our mothers or fathers takes us somewhere in the car (we're not old enough to drive) and we get so wrapped up in what we're saying that we just forget anyone else is around. I can see it is rude, but what can I do about it?

Ginger

Dear Ginger,

I know this is something my friends and I tended to do as teen-agers. Sometimes you forget to appreciate other people, but there is never any excuse for poor manners and that is just what you and your friends are displaying.

When you come into your home with friends, pause a moment and say, "Hi, Mom. The craziest thing happened at school . . ." and tell her some event of the day, briefly, before you move on. The other girls will soon catch on and probably join in on the story themselves.

At someone else's house, you can always say, "Hello, Mrs. Curtis. How are you?" and add any personal observation that you can. If she's knitting, you might show interest in what she's making. Or if she's reading a book, ask about it. Any parent will appreciate youthful interest in his or her activities.

And it's so important to express appreciation—just a simple "thank you," sincerely spoken, will make adults respect you. Some of these common courtesies could build rapport that would carry over into other situations, too.

If you start it, wherever you go, it's bound to catch on and your friends will do it. It's important in life—being appreciative, saying thank you and just being friendly to people.

Vonda Kay

Dear Vonda Kay,

My friends call me "The Brain" because I get good grades. I have to work hard for what I get and inside I'm proud. But the teasing gets kind of rough. Why do average kids want to ridicule the better students? No one teases the athletes or the good musicians.

Crystal

Dear Crystal,

Someone once told me that if people tease you, it's because they like you. If they don't like you, they won't bother to tease you.

Hard as it is to understand and accept, some of their ridiculing may stem from just plain jealousy. Every student would like to make good grades and, rather than admit their disappointment with the ones they get, they take it out on you.

You don't sound like the kind of girl who brags or tries to show off intelligence, but I'll just add a word of caution. Your own attitude makes a lot of difference, too. Nothing is more irritating to the average student than to hear The Brain saying "Oh, I flunked, I know I did" and then pull an A. Or if a test was easy for you and others are complaining about how hard it was, be careful not to blurt out, "I thought it was simple." Either say nothing or comment on some question that seemed tricky or perhaps stumped even you.

Enter into extracurricular activities as much as possible so you can compete with the others in situations where some of their skills may very well outshine yours.

I'm sure it's hard to anticipate now, but the fact that you've learned to work hard will put you well out in front later on—and there won't be any teasing then.

Vonda Kay

Dear Vonda Kay,

A boy from our school is in the service. He graduated last year and is two years older than I am. I always sort of liked him, but he didn't pay any attention to me. His sister says he is lonely and homesick. Would it be all right to write to him? Even if he hasn't written first?

Harriet

Dear Harriet,

I think it would be a wonderful idea to write your friend who is in the service. It's so important to servicemen to hear from folks at home. It's one way we can support them and share in what they're doing. If there is some club in your school that would do it, you might try to interest them in a letter-writing project and write to all recent graduates who are in the armed services, especially those overseas.

In your particular case, I would suggest that you be very newsy about school events, what's going on in your town, activities of friends whom he may have known, funny stories about teachers, books you're reading, etc. Keep the tone of your letters gay and cheerful.

It is easy to get personal in letters. You feel you can say things that you might never say in the person's presence. Don't be sentimental or express the attraction you once felt for him. If your correspondence continues, he just might look you up when he comes home and then you can decide how you feel.

So—do write. Everyone likes to get letters!

Vonda Kay

Dear Vonda Kay,

I am a good student and get top grades. But this year I have a teacher that I just can't stand. She doesn't like me either and is giving me the lowest grades I've ever had in my whole life. I just don't know how to get along with her or what to do.

Carole

Dear Carole,

All through life we come up against people with whom we just seem to clash. It may be a classmate, a neighbor, a business associate or even sometimes a boss. In your case, it had to be a teacher on whom you have to depend for a grade. That doesn't seem fair when a whole year's work is involved, or when it means a job promotion or some other important thing. But it happens—and this won't be the last time.

There are two things you can do about it. You can just give up and quit trying, take the poor grade and always excuse yourself by saying, "Well, the teacher didn't like me."

Or you can take it as a challenge and try to figure out ways to come out on top of the situation.

Let me give a personal example. In high school I was very much interested in speech classes and so that became my major the first two years in college. But I had a teacher that I just didn't feel was giving me a fair shake. I tried hard but it always seemed that, no matter what I came up with, I couldn't please her. So every time I had to give a speech, I spent twice as much time preparing it as I had before. I'd hunt up more examples to illustrate my points. It was hard work, but, you know, I think I learned twice as much in that class, because of my effort, than I ever did in any other speech class.

I was terribly disappointed in my C grade—the only C I ever had in my college major—but I surely learned a lot. And I went right back to A's again in subsequent classes.

Since you can't change the situation and you're going to have to put up with this teacher for a year, you'd better not lose the whole year's work by brooding about it. Do your best, no matter what the results are. Take the grade you're given, but get something out of the course.

Vonda Kay

Dear Vonda Kay,

What experiences do you remember most about your year as Miss America? Would you advise pretty girls to try out for such contests?

Julie

Dear Julie,

If I were to try to write about all the wonderful experiences that were mine during that memorable year, I think I could fill up about twenty million pages! I had so many experiences that still mean a great deal to me and are such treasured memories of that entire year.

The travel was an inspiring part of that experience. The money and gifts were most welcome, and I enjoyed the excitement of being in the spotlight. But the *most* important? That which has lasted longest and meant the most to me are all the wonderful friends I made during that year.

The other day I emceed a beauty pageant in North Carolina. The judges weren't quite ready with their decision, so I had to ad lib for a bit and I said something like this: "You know, when these girls go home they will have memories of the bright spotlight, the orchestra music, and all the excitement of the pageantry. They will have a feeling of accomplishment from the applause of the audience. But the spotlight soon grows dim in their minds and the music fades away and there is no audience applause. Then they will know that what the pageant really meant to them is having this opportunity to meet and know all the wonderful people here at the pageant. Each one who has an open mind and open heart takes something back with her that another gave. And each one gives something of herself to others."

58

Would I advise pretty girls to enter such contests? A pretty girl is not necessarily a prospective winner if she goes on a pretty face alone. She must have personality and talent to go with it. The talent need not be some fantastic or unusual ability, but it must be presented well. One Miss America demonstrated her sewing in a unique and interesting way and completely captivated her audience and the judges.

It takes a friendly personality to really show off a pretty face. A sincere and happy smile, a desire to win but a willingness to accept the fact that you may not, and a purpose deeper than just glory for yourself—if you possess these qualities, I would recommend that you try out. Whether you reach the top or not, the experience is a worthwhile one.

Vonda Kay

4

Go Steady? ... Make Out? ...

Dating or "going out with," as most of you express it, is an important part of growing up. Besides all the fun and enjoyment, it serves some more serious and valuable purposes.

You have a good opportunity to study yourself and see how you act with different people—if you are a better, kinder person for being with them or if you become a more selfish one. You will see, too, what effect you have on others.

This is a good time to think about your values and your goals in life, how important your religion is to you, how well you can handle difficult situations, and how strong you are in the face of temptation.

You will also begin to understand what love is and that it includes thoughtfulness, understanding and unselfishness. When you like someone very much, that person's happiness will come before your own. Not that you'll marry the first person you date, nor even the first person you "fall in love with," but you will begin to learn about love and your own reactions and feelings.

Dear Vonda Kay,
  What age do you think girls should start going out with boys?

  Jackie

Dear Jackie,

If you are hoping I will say fourteen, maybe even twelve, you will be disappointed. I couldn't possibly name a specific age at which every girl should suddenly have her first date.

When *you're* old enough is the right time—and I don't mean your next birthday or even your last one. I'm thinking of emotional age, and there are at least two ways you'll recognize it.

First of all, you'll be wanting to go out and not doing it just because it's expected. Boys will become an attraction to you instead of a big nuisance. You'll begin to care how you look and act when they're around. Somehow I rather suspect you have reached this stage.

But secondly, the right time will be when your parents feel you are mature enough to know how to conduct yourself with a boy. This will depend on the way you assume responsibility around the house, how you talk in conversations about boys and dating, whether you seem to recognize right and wrong in other situations.

I think my first date was after my eighth-grade graduation and it was a very closely chaperoned affair. I really began to date in high school, and I did it with my parents' approval.

It helps, too, if your parents know the boy you are going out with and if he is around your age. I think that dating older fellows might cause your parents to worry more, especially if you are just starting to go out.

Try to get tuned in with your folks' way of thinking at the start, talking over your plans and working out problems together. It will make it easier for you later on.

Vonda Kay

Dear Vonda Kay,

Do you believe in love at first sight? I met this guy at a school mixer and I just fell hard. Of course, we're pretty young, fifteen and sixteen, but it does happen that way sometimes, doesn't it?

Lauren

Dear Lauren,

I suppose I do believe in love at first sight—at fifteen years of age. It happened to you, didn't it? I'm afraid it's not the most lasting kind of love and the "breaking up" is just as painful as the "falling in" is ecstatic. So take it slowly and keep your feet on the ground.

Vonda Kay

Dear Vonda Kay,

I feel like a real nut writing to you, but I did hear you speak once and you sound like you're okay.

You see, there's this girl at school. A real doll, you know. Figure. Looks. Clothes. You name it, she has it. Anyhow, I'd sure like to take her out sometime. But she has this thing for the big football heroes and doesn't even look at anybody else. What makes girls go for the big-shouldered type? They're great on the football field, but outside of that they're not much. Since you're a girl, maybe you can explain what is so great about the athletes and what a guy like me (I can walk on my hands) can do to attract some attention.

Phil

Dear Phil,

I suppose a fellow does feel a little "like a nut" when writing for advice. I'm glad you did, though, because your particular question came at exactly the right time for me.

63

I have just been visiting with one of my high school girl friends and we were talking about our dating days and what we looked for in our high school boy friends. I'm afraid I'll have to admit that I was a bit like the gal you want to take out—and your question helps me to see the other side.

You see, the girls who are really with it, so to speak, the real dolls who wear the nice clothes and always look good, are many times interested only in furthering themselves. One way to do that is to go out with someone who also stands out and looks good—like the big football hero.

As my friend and I talked on, we recalled how we felt about boys in high school. We had tended to be more interested in the positions they held than in the fellows' personalities. We thought it was exciting to go with a football player—or a basketball star, a track man or the student body president. It was a boost for our egos, you know, to go with those fellows.

We both had certain standards that we felt the boys we dated must meet, but I can tell you that if we put a football player side by side with a good student and both had the same personal standards, the football player would score higher.

I think now that this was an indication of immaturity on our part. As we went on into college, we stopped judging a person on what he did and started looking at what he was. We started to think about things like preparing for marriage and what kind of a person we would want to live with the rest of our lives. And we had some doubts about those high school heroes; maybe on the football field they were pretty sharp, but how would they be around the house? And now as I look at the adults whom I most admire, I have no idea if they played football in high school or not and I really don't care.

Now, Phil, I've admitted that this is immature on the girl's part, but how about you? Look at the qualities you listed that attract you to her—a real doll, figure, looks, clothes and all. Aren't you doing just exactly what she is? She's out for the hero-image and you for the glamor-type. I hope you both soon discover that the truly important thing in life is what a person *is* and not what he *does*. Maybe then, who knows, you two just might get along beautifully.

Vonda Kay

P.S. Would you believe I married an ex-football player?

Dear Vonda Kay,
What can a girl say when turning down a kiss on a first date? Especially if she wants the guy to come around again.

Grace

Dear Grace,
When you sense the moment is approaching, you'd better give his hand a warm squeeze, tell him what a lovely time you had, say a sweet "goodnight" and slip into the house.

If he asks you for a kiss, why not just answer in as friendly a way as possible, "Oh, let's save that for another time." It's worth a try.

Vonda Kay

Dear Vonda Kay,
Do you think a girl of fifteen should go steady? If you say no, would you tell me what age you do think is old enough? I am a responsible girl.

Emmy

Dear Emmy,
How old should a person be to go steady? It's almost like asking—how long is a string? Some twenty-five-year-olds aren't old enough and some girls younger than you are might be able to handle it.

I think it's a pretty serious step to cut yourself off from all other

65

friendships and see one boy exclusively. I never went steady in high school and I'm glad I didn't. Though I dated one fellow quite a lot, there was no "steady" understanding. Here are my reasons for opposing steady dating in high school:

You are tied to just one person and are not free to get to know others. If you do talk to someone else, jealousy enters the picture and someone gets angry. Also, going steady often leads to intimacies that high school girls should avoid. When you see one boy exclusively, you make it hard for yourself.

Then, if you never go steady, you don't have to break up. I saw so many depressed and unhappy girls who had just "broken up" that I never wanted to go through it.

You may think there is some security in knowing you'll have a regular weekend date or someone to take you to the prom, but you also miss much of the excitement of getting a surprise phone call and of getting to know new people.

I'm glad you are a responsible girl, Emmy, and I just hope you stay that way as you make your decision about going steady.

Vonda Kay

Dear Vonda Kay,

What kind of gift is appropriate for a sixteen-year-old girl to give a boy for his birthday? I really like him and have been saving for something special.

Kati

Dear Kati,

Expensive or very personal gifts are certainly not to be considered appropriate for teen-age giving. I'd suggest a tie tack or perhaps a wallet with his name inside. Clothing seems too personal a gift. You shouldn't spend a large sum of money—that makes it awkward for him when your birthday rolls around.

Something cute, like a different kind of piggy bank or a little ornament to put in his car, or maybe his favorite record album or a book by an author he admires, are other ideas. Keep your

66

ears open when you're together and he may unknowingly suggest just the right thing.

Vonda Kay

Dear Vonda Kay,
 Should a girl settle for second best or always wait for her ideal? I mean about boy friends. Seems like the creeps ask me out and the guys I really like don't even know I'm around.

Deedee

Dear Deedee,
 By "second best" I'm assuming you mean nice fellows, just not the most popular and athletic type. If by "creeps" you mean the black-jacketed motorcycle crowd, I'd say, "No, never settle for second best."

 But if it's just because they are not class leaders or are maybe the studious type, my advice is—accept dates with them. Be glad someone is asking you out. If you get a reputation for being lots of fun and a good sport, the word will get around and some of those dream guys will start looking you up.

 Maybe you are setting your sights too high. There is nothing more futile than a freshman drooling over a senior. True, those romances do happen, but oh, so very seldom. Some girls spend hours just daydreaming about their Prince Charming and then no other boy looks good to them. Check your sights, Deedee, and be sure you're shooting within range.

Vonda Kay

Dear Vonda Kay,
 I'm an honor student, a junior in high school and very much interested in art. Tommy is a senior and just about the greatest. We have so many things in common. He plans to be a commercial artist and has already won several blue ribbons in contests

and exhibits he's entered. We like the same music, books, every-
thing. But there's one big problem—our religions. My parents are
terribly strict and when they found out what he is they told me
not to go out with him or even talk with him on the phone. I love
my parents and I believe deeply in my religion, but aren't they
being prejudiced about this? What can I do?

Kathy

Dear Kathy,

You and Tommy do have lots of interests in common and as you match them up, it almost sounds like you are trying to match for more than just a few weeks or months, and more than just casual dating. This is probably what is upsetting your parents. The religious factor is so important in any relationship of value that they are justly concerned, not prejudiced, as you suggest in your letter.

In my own dating days, I didn't even want to go out with any-one who wasn't at least of a similar faith to mine. I, too, was raised in quite a strict home, but in my case I never rebelled against my parents' wishes, because I felt deeply about the importance of my religion. I don't mean within denominations, but the basic faith or lack of any faith at all.

I know that at your age you're not thinking of marriage, yet you never know which friendship is going to develop into that most serious step of all—marriage. There is a saying, "Every date—a potential mate." This may well be your parents' concern —and I wouldn't call them prejudiced or bigoted for it.

Frankly, I always tried to avoid the situation you are in by just not accepting the first date with anyone whose religion I could not agree with, or someone who had no religion at all.

Your parents are only looking out for your ultimate happiness. They seem hard and inflexible to you now—as in so many conflicts between young people and their parents. All too often teen-agers make some defiant move against their parents at such a time and do something they may later be sorry for. I just wish there were statistics for the number of times that young folks

68

have said, "I wish I had listened to you." So—respect your parents' wishes and don't judge them too harshly.

Vonda Kay

Dear Vonda Kay,

Sometimes I think a girl has to make out to be popular with the boys. I just don't care for it and think there are many other ways to have fun. But I don't think my ideas are so good, because I'm not getting asked out. Should I think this over a bit more, do you think?

Evie

Dear Evie,

You just might be making an error in the reason that you are not being asked out. It could be that something is lacking in your personality and it's not your unwillingness to "make out" at all.

If you are very friendly and sweet and loads of fun on a date, you're going to be asked out again. You don't have to be cold when refusing a kiss. That can be done in a sweet, kind way. It's the gal who freezes and says a curt "no" who gets the title of "cold fish."

I agree with your reasoning and hope you don't change your standards of conduct. There won't be any need to if you go to work on improving your personality.

Vonda Kay

Dear Vonda Kay,

My boy friend just told me we are through. We went steady for almost a year and I just can't stand it. I can't eat or sleep and I cry over any little thing. My mother keeps saying it was just puppy love and I'll get over it. But I don't see how I ever will. He's going with another girl now and I get sick when I see them together. I try never to meet him in the hall because I don't think I could even speak to him. I'm afraid to turn the radio on because I hear records that we used to like, together. It's just a terrible feeling and I don't know what to do. I'm sure I'll always love him.

Jenny Sue

Dear Jenny Sue,

I doubt if there's much I can say in the way of consolation that would be of any help. You're going through an experience that most girls face sometime in their lives, and I can understand your feelings exactly. You're suffering and it's a terrible feeling. Your parents are hurting, too, and I can imagine your friends hear a sad story from you—everyone feels badly along with you except the former boy friend, who seems to be doing all right.

Okay, I'd say—enough! Self-pity, starvation and tears won't get you anywhere. Maybe it was puppy love, maybe it wasn't. But whatever it was, it's obviously not going anywhere. So put it behind you—and believe it or not, that is possible.

Pray about it: the Lord gives strength when you run out of it. Then get up from your knees, dry your eyes, fix your face, comb your hair and go meet the gang. Join in the fun—look for new boy friends. Focus your attention on other things and forget your sorrow (that is, if you're not enjoying it too much). Sometime, Jenny Sue, you'll be the one to say if this was puppy love or not.

Vonda Kay

Dear Vonda Kay,

Would you tell me how I can suggest helping to pay for a date? I like a guy whose family doesn't have any extra money and I know that my allowance is much bigger than his. Would I hurt his pride if I suggested helping in some way?

Michelle

70

Dear Michelle,

It's certainly considerate of you to want to help out, but it's a touchy situation. A boy takes pride in being able to take his girl out and you must be careful not to destroy that.

There are several ways I think of in which you might be able to help out without offending. Occasionally invite him to have dinner at your house. Maybe ask him to go on a family outing now and then. Be careful not to order expensive foods when he does take you out. Suggest activities that cost little or nothing. Maybe your parents could pick up tickets to something special and casually suggest that the two of you could use a couple of them if you wanted.

If you really like him, you'll respect his male pride and handle the situation with tender, loving care.

Vonda Kay

Dear Vonda Kay,

Is it ever proper for a girl to offer the use of her car for a date? I have offered several times—my folks don't mind—but my boy friend seems embarrassed. Isn't it better than walking or staying home?

Bonnie

Dear Bonnie,

Surely you've answered your own question. Your boy friend seems embarrassed—isn't that enough?

It was all right to offer the first time. If he had accepted with ease, then you could have done it on other occasions.

But if he's embarrassed about it, then forget it. Anyway, walking is healthy and it can be enjoyable if you're holding hands with a fellow you like. Don't make him feel as if it's a terrible sacrifice for you to go on foot occasionally.

Vonda Kay

Dear Vonda Kay,

What do you think of drive-in movie dates? My folks do not approve and I know a lot of making out goes on. But I'm not like that.

Kathleen

Dear Kathleen,

I do not think much of drive-in movies for high school dates. You know why as well as I do. You may not be "like that" but you could spend a couple of uncomfortable hours fighting off someone who is. Do your movie-going at indoor theaters and avoid temptation and the bad reputation that comes from going to drive-ins. Choose a good picture—and enjoy *it*.

Vonda Kay

Dear Vonda Kay,

A couple we like to double with goes pretty heavy on this making-out business. I'm pretty firm about not doing it, but my boy friend says it makes us look pretty kiddish to just sit with his arm around me or hold hands. Maybe he is right?

Tracey

Dear Tracey,

When a couple is pressured into breaking down their standards because of their double date, it's time to change your dating doubles. It appears you aren't having much influence on *them*, so break away before they have an influence on you.

Vonda Kay

Dear Vonda Kay,

My boy friend and I are both Christian young people and go to church regularly. We're very much in love and have been *going steady for almost six months. We're both seniors in high school. We are alone a lot, in the car especially, and have been doing some petting. Sometimes I feel guilty but he says if we're in love it's all right. I do love him and I want to do the things we're doing, too. I just can't seem to stop either. It isn't as if we're free with just anybody, only with each other. Do you think this is so serious? We will get married someday.*

Helen

Dear Helen,

You end your letter with that definite statement, "We will get married. . . ." I wonder how many times a young person has said that. You are one more couple among the many teen-agers who make marriage plans before they are mature enough to do so. I know that our society is partly responsible for causing young people to think about marriage before they are really prepared for it. If you wait just a few years, even two years of college, you may have a very different idea of the kind of person you want to spend a lifetime with.

Now—the real problem. Yes, I do think your situation and this whole problem of petting are very serious. Just because you are not free with everyone does not make your present situation right. You are treading on very dangerous ground. Your emotions just may win over your knowledge of right and wrong, and you will find yourselves in real trouble and being forced into a marriage you are not ready for.

Why must you be alone so much? Can't you join other couples for an evening of fun? Or even go to one of your homes and be with your families for TV or some of the fun games that folks are enjoying now. You yourself recognize how real this temptation is, so why don't you make an effort to avoid being alone in the car or anywhere else?

You are already feeling guilty. Pretty soon you'll have to lie about what you're doing. You won't respect yourself or your boy friend any more. You're playing with explosives, Helen, and you seem to know it, too, or you wouldn't have written to me. The

73

only safe and right thing to do is to make a change. Please do it before you lose your self-respect.

Vonda Kay

Dear Vonda Kay,

You talk to so many girls, maybe you can help me. I'm going to be seventeen in another month and have a baby a month later. I had read about the dangers of petting but I thought we could stop before we went too far. Well, we didn't. Here I am and no one can possibly know how terrible it's been. There's not much point in going into all the details but we didn't get married and I'm not going to keep the baby. It will go to some couple who will love it and be better parents than my boy friend and I would have been (only he's not even a boy friend anymore).

How can I ever make it up to my family? I have a sister in college and a brother in high school. My parents are both active in church and I have always been, too. They've all been great, but I've hurt them terribly. Will we ever get over the disgrace and what can I do?

Darien

Dear Darien,

I just wish I could send a copy of your letter to every girl who asks me what I think of petting. If they could just see what heartache it can lead to, they wouldn't even be debating the issue.

Darien, you are so fortunate to have such a wonderful family standing behind you. Obviously they love you very much and want to help you. You've made a costly mistake, but it needn't ruin the lives of everyone about you—nor your own.

What you do when this is all over is important. Finish your school and go on to college. Make something out of your life and give your family reason to have had faith in you.

In the meantime, be helpful and cooperative at home. Try to be cheerful even though you may not feel that way. Don't brood

74

about your wrongdoing or spend time feeling sorry for yourself.

Jesus taught a way of love and forgiveness, and your family has followed it. Accept it with deepest gratitude and humility— and go on from there.

Vonda Kay

5

My Use of the Family Car

A year or more before you got your license, you probably started marking off the days on the calendar and dreaming of the day when you would drive off alone and take the gang for a ride.

Then, bang, you get your license and it isn't at all as you had dreamed it would be. Those car keys aren't yours for the asking and all kinds of unexpected conflicts arise.

Just take it easy. It takes time for parents to get used to the idea that their "child" is capable of driving, especially if you're the first in the family to do so.

As you prove your ability and dependability, the situation will smooth out. Try to plan ahead and to keep communication lines open. If you act responsibly in other situations, your parents will consider you capable in this one.

Dear Vonda Kay,

My mother won't let me go on car dates. I am almost fifteen and my boy friend has his license. It is very awkward, since he can drive and I can't ride. What can I do?

Sharon

Dear Sharon,

You can do just what your mother asks you to. She reads the daily newspaper and sees the horrible pictures of accidents in almost every edition. Because she cares about you and doesn't want anything to happen to you, she has made a rule.

Tell your boy friend to watch his reputation as a driver. If someone tells your mother how careful he is, she may begin to change her mind. Ask for short trips at first—like the nearest ice-cream spot or some event at school or church.

As she gets used to it and he proves himself—and you turn fifteen—maybe things will change.

Vonda Kay

Dear Vonda Kay,

I have had my driver's license for a few months now and my father is quite generous about the car. But I'm not supposed to let anyone else drive it. What do I tell my girl when she begs me to teach her to drive? It's rough, because I want to do what my dad asks, but I also sure like my girl.

Dennis

Dear Dennis,

I wish I could write to your girl friend instead of you. She is being very selfish to beg you to do something your father has requested you not to.

Your dad is being cooperative in letting you use the car; you must be just as cooperative in observing the rules he lays down. Explain to her that you have the car with the understanding that no one else is to drive it. "I know you'll understand how it is," might help.

Be firm. If you can't keep this gal without giving in on driving, I think you'd better look for someone who's interested in you— and not your car.

Vonda Kay

Dear Vonda Kay,

In my state we can't drive till we're seventeen. What's a guy to do when there's a real special party? My father and mother say they'll chauffeur me, but I'd feel like a kid.

Ron

Dear Ron,

I surely can't blame you for not wanting to use your dad as chauffeur on a special occasion. I see only two other solutions, however. One is to ask an older friend to let you double or triple date with him. We used to do this and it was always a lot more fun to go someplace afterwards when we were all in formals or special attire, if we were in a group. You should offer to help on the gas or whatever arrangement he has for the car's use.

The other possibility is to use a taxi. That can really add up, but kids in the cities often do it for special occasions. Again, it helps to split the bill with another couple.

If your father does have to do the driving and he is a wise father, he will realize he's playing the part of chauffeur and will enter into the conversation only if it seems natural to do so.

And cheer up, Ron, every day is one day nearer that seventeenth birthday.

Vonda Kay

Dear Vonda Kay,

I have my driver's license now and often want the car for just little errands. My folks have said I can have it once a weekend only. How unreasonable can they get? The car is just sitting there —they aren't going anyplace. But no, I can't have it. I don't get their reasoning, if it can be called that.

Brenda

Dear Brenda,

Did you ask your parents about their reasons? Sometimes teen-agers blow their tops without seriously trying to discover what Dad and Mom have in mind.

I'm just guessing—but maybe they worry about you when you're out. Do they feel you are a responsible driver? If not, it could be they want to give you a little more time to grow up. If you are just starting to drive, don't push them. They have to get used to the idea and then they'll come through.

Maybe you're the kind who makes unreasonable requests for the car and rather than decide each time, they made a cover-all rule. Then, too, it costs something each time the car is driven. Not just the gas, there's wear and tear put on with every mile. They may be thinking of this.

Even though my family had two cars, it was not always con-venient for me to take one when I wanted to. I had saved my money since I was a young girl so I went out and bought my own car. It cost $250 or $300 and I had to spend an additional $50 to have a mechanic check it over. It wasn't any real beauty —except to me. But I was so proud of it and gave it the best of care. Maybe you should start saving and planning toward your own.

In the meantime, talk it over with your folks. Maybe you can find a compromise that will make everybody happy.

Vonda Kay

Dear Vonda Kay,

I'm just about ready to get my driver's license and already I
see trouble ahead. I said something about driving the girls somewhere—whew, the roof just about caved in. "If you think you're
going to get the car for every little thing" and "That car is a
powerful piece of machinery," etc., etc., etc. What's the point in
getting a license with parents like that? I'm not wild or anything
and I believe I'm going to be a good driver. How do I handle
this situation?

Ellie

Dear Ellie,

Probably part of the problem is that you don't have your
license yet and so your parents don't really think of you as a
qualified driver. During the time you drive with just a permit, a
licensed driver will have to be with you. This is a good time to
show your parents that you are a competent driver. If they want
to-go to the store, ask if you might do the driving. Then listen
respectfully to their suggestions and never argue with them about
driving rules or techniques. Be calm and confident as you drive.
This will instill confidence in them, too.

Once you prove you are a skillful driver and have your license,
then go at things slowly. It's as hard for parents to see their kids
take off alone in a car as it is for you to keep from asking for it
every minute. Balance out your requests for its use. Maybe you
can arrive at some agreement as to how often you can use it.
Whatever you do, be home exactly at the hour agreed upon, because something in parents really makes them worry.

Remember, the car is theirs. They paid for it and they take
care of it. If you have too much conflict, you may want to start
saving for one of your own. When it's *your* car, you'll realize why
they are so cautious with theirs.

It's not just the car, either—though it may seem that way to
you. They're concerned about you, because they love you and

don't want anything to happen to you. Remember that when you feel the roof caving in.

Vonda Kay

Dear Vonda Kay,

What makes some boys get so show-offish when they get behind the wheel? Even my boy friend, who is usually rather quiet and very well-mannered, goes too fast, screeches the tires and tries to pass everything on the road. Honestly, sometimes I'm actually scared. Why must he—and what does a gal who likes him do?

Meri

Dear Meri,

I don't understand either what makes some boys become such show-offs behind the wheel. You'd think they'd want to take better care of the car and put an even higher value on the lives of those in the car. One reason for their actions might be that they are hoping to impress you. Simply let them know you're unimpressed.

I can't tell you exactly why they do it, but I certainly know that I wouldn't remain very long in a car that's being driven that way. You should make it clear that you don't go for reckless driving. Either it stops or you get out. Maybe your firm action can prevent some serious disaster.

Vonda Kay

6

Money Problems

According to national statistics, teen-agers have fantastic amounts of money to spend. So how is it that "I never seem to have enough"?

Money always seems to go faster than we want it to. Ask your parents. They probably have their problems with it, too, and it isn't especially helpful to have every member of the family clamoring for more.

As you do begin to earn a little cash, plan for its use with care. Again, you develop habits now that will either help or hinder later on when you're trying to balance that all-important family budget.

While you're starting to use your own money you'll learn many valuable lessons that will aid you later. One habit that is good for you to establish is that of designating your money for different areas, such as clothing, entertainment, and—how about a tithe to the church? I started this when I was young, because I have always felt that a tenth of all I earn or am given belongs to God. After all, it really *all* belongs to Him and we are only given its use. I hope you remember to include Him in your personal budget, too.

Dear Vonda Kay,

My parents don't seem to realize how much it costs a teen-ager to get along these days. Just to take a girl out to the movies is more than my whole week's allowance. Yet Dad says this is already more than a guy needs. What should a boy's allowance be? And while you're on it, my sisters get the same amount that I do. Is this fair? They say their make-up, etc. (whatever etc. is) costs them as much as my dates do me.

Pete

Dear Pete,

It is expensive to take a girl out, I agree with you 100 per cent. *But* what makes you think your dad should work hard so you can take a girl out and have a good time? Your dad is doing you a favor and I think he's wise. If you need more cash, you get out and work a little for it. There's a wide choice of jobs for the guy who really wants to earn—delivering papers, raking leaves, caring for lawns, and for you Illinois fellows, I understand there's plenty of snow to shovel.

Be thankful for what you're getting free—someone had to work for it, you know—and dig in on your own for any more that you need. You may be a little more careful how you spend it when you have to earn it.

I'm not going to suggest a definite amount that I think you should have for an allowance. It depends on so many circumstances that I don't know about—like how much your family can give without sacrificing something else, what the alternatives are for less expensive entertainment, and what you are expected to use your allowance for. Allowances vary a lot among teen-agers that I know. Some don't get a regular allowance but have to ask each time they need something.

This has to be worked out in each individual family and I'd suggest that you and your sisters accept with gratitude what your parents give. If you don't like it, you're the one to do something about it (besides complaining).

Vonda Kay

Dear Vonda Kay,

I baby-sit a lot. It doesn't pay as much as some jobs but I can study while I'm there. Since I earn the money I get, shouldn't I be the one who says how I spend it? My folks are always saying I should save it. Or they don't like something I buy with it. I feel this way: I work and earn it, so it's mine. Right or wrong?

Yvonne

Dear Yvonne,

Baby-sitting has been the teen-age girl's lifesaver as far as earning money is concerned. It is an ideal first job for girls and it surely helps financially.

Now, I must say I think both you *and* your parents are right. It is your money and you should have the final say on how it is used. But you should think through your expenditures very carefully. They are wise in asking you to save a little of it. Why don't you set up a savings plan, putting a certain part of what you earn in the bank? Someday you'll have it for that something special you want very much. You'll also be developing a habit of not spending every cent you earn, which will help you all your life.

I remember the very first money I earned as a little girl. I didn't want to spend it. I saved it and saved it and saved it. Saving became a habit with me and I have been grateful for it many times since.

You also might ease the situation by discussing with your parents your expected expenditures. Get their advice occasionally. Once they feel you're using your money wisely, they won't even question you. It's amazing how valuable parents' experience can be, and their advice is well worth listening to.

Vonda Kay

Dear Vonda Kay,

You being a girl and all, maybe you can give me an idea how to let a girl know when a guy doesn't have much money to blow on an evening's entertainment? I'm badly limited and can barely get enough for a show, let alone the food afterwards, and the gas (I always pay my dad for that).

Robbie

Dear Robbie,

I don't know how well you know the girl—but some fellows I know make sort of a joke out of it and actually tell a girl when they ask for the date "I've got exactly four dollars. Let's see what kind of an evening we can have on that."

However, it takes a certain kind of person to pull that one off. Many fellows would find that approach embarrassing. You might pick her up a little later so you'll only have time for a quick soda after the movie.

Frankly, girls are often bewildered when it comes to ordering. If you'd just say, "How about a hot fudge sundae?" that gives a cue as to what you have to spend. If she doesn't like hot fudge sundaes, a girl with any common sense will order something comparable in price.

And—that's very thoughtful of you, to pay your dad for gas!

Vonda Kay

Dear Vonda Kay,

Should parents cut off a kid's allowance just because she's earning money? I have a good part-time waitress job and I'm buying some nice clothes. The other day my dad said if I could afford things like that, he couldn't see why I needed an allowance. And that was that. Just because I have some ambition, should that change things?

Lynn

86

Dear Lynn,

I have a feeling that the question stems from the way you are using your money and not from your dad's really wanting to cut off your allowance. He's either not pleased because you are buying too many clothes or else you are buying such expensive ones that he doesn't approve. You are to be commended on your ambition, true, but how about your wisdom in the use of money?

Maybe you could suggest that your allowance go into a savings account for your college education or some other specific goal. If your father feels you are handling money wisely, he may not be so inclined to withhold your allowance.

Vonda Kay

Dear Vonda Kay,

My mother doesn't especially like to shop for me—we disagree on most choices. So I suggested she just let me use her charge plate. She won't even listen. She pays for it anyway, why not let me be independent?

Marti

Dear Marti,

A charge plate is just a little like a blank check made out to you. It's a big responsibility—and a temptation to spend unlimited amounts. Although you may be perfectly trustworthy, I feel that's too much freedom for a young girl.

I had a system worked out with my parents that gave me independence and also taught me something about budgeting. In college—before I began working—my parents gave me five dollars a week for clothing. Well, as you can imagine, I soon discovered that five dollars didn't go very far by itself, but $10 or $15 would, and five dollars a week equalled $20 a month. So if there was a dress or a pair of shoes I wanted, I knew I had to plan ahead. Sometimes I found I needed still more and so I took baby-sitting jobs to bring in that extra revenue.

87

This is one way and it worked well for me. Maybe you and your mother can work out some other arrangement that is satisfactory to you both. Decide on something together and then stick by it. Don't ask for exceptions to the rule. One of the best ways to be independent is to show that you are capable of handling the freedom you are given.

Vonda Kay

Dear Vonda Kay,

Most kids' folks give them a lump sum of money for Christmas present buying. My folks won't kick in a cent more than my usual allowance. They say I should save all year from my allowance. It's too small as it is. Shouldn't parents help out with something extra at Christmas?

Jo Ellen

Dear Jo Ellen,

Christmas is the time of year for fun and surprises. It's the time to give out of love and happiness. Somehow I can't see your idea of saying, "Hey, Dad. How about some money to buy you a present?" That isn't really giving, now is it?

Even if the gift is insignificant as far as purchase price is concerned, it will mean more to the receiver if you handle it all on your own.

Start preparing for Christmas from three to six months ahead of time. You can either buy a gift every couple of weeks to put away and have ready, or save a little cash regularly. If you can't seem to leave your home savings bank alone, why not try opening a Christmas account in a bank? You can open one with as little as fifty cents a week and that would be a nice lump sum to have when December rolls around.

Don't forget, Jo Ellen, what Christmas is all about. Give happiness and love along with your material gift.

Vonda Kay

Dear Vonda Kay,

I have a friend who is always borrowing money. It may just be a quarter or fifty cents, but once she borrowed two dollars. She seems to forget all about it. Once I reminded her and she got mad and said, "What do you think I am—I pay my debts." She still hasn't paid me back.

Alyce

Dear Alyce,

I think it was Shakespeare who said, "Neither a borrower nor a lender be; for loan oft loses both itself and friend." How very wise he was. Why don't you just mark off that two dollars as "paid for a lesson well learned"? And say no next time. Friendships are for sharing many things, but money isn't among them.

Vonda Kay

7

I've Got a Job . . .

Even the smallest job you are willing to tackle will help prepare for real wage-earning positions later in life. But in every instance, you must work hard to prove you are responsible enough for the job you have.

You form habits, good and bad, from the first hour of your employment. If you "goof off" and try to do as little real work as you can get away with, you're soon going to have to start taking second-rate jobs. On the other hand, a dependable person will always be in line for better jobs and better pay.

A part-time job can be of help, too, as you plan your life's vocation. It gives you the opportunity to study yourself and your own special aptitudes. If at all possible, try to find jobs that are similar to or will help you prepare for the vocation you're looking toward. At any rate, just learning to take orders cheerfully, to complete jobs you start and to show you are dependable are all wonderful training for future full-time employment.

So set that alarm clock, be on time, and show your employer (including the mothers for whom you baby-sit) that you can be counted on.

Dear Vonda Kay,

I've got to get a summer job but the interviews have me scared to death. Can you suggest something that will make me more confident?

Tonia

Dear Tonia,

Interviews used to scare me, too, I must admit. Maybe a little personal pep talk outside the door will build up your confidence. Tell yourself, "I know I can do the job. I can do it better than many of the others he is interviewing. I have certain qualities that qualify me for this position," etc. Then keep it all in mind as you go in the door.

It's a good idea to know the interviewer's name so you can address him properly. Be prepared to ask intelligent questions about what's expected of you and to state clearly your own abilities (not that personal pep talk, however, it's just a bit too egotistical). Dress in good taste: nothing extreme either in clothes or make-up. Don't chew gum.

If you find you are terribly nervous, you might frankly tell him, "This is my first interview and to tell the truth, I'm a little afraid." He'll probably laugh with you and try to put you at ease.

Good luck and I hope you get a job you like.

Vonda Kay

Dear Vonda Kay,

Is it all right to exaggerate your abilities just a little when applying for a job? Jobs aren't that easy to get, with so much competition, and if you know you could do it, couldn't you just say you do to get the job?

Marla

Dear Marla,

I'm afraid I don't follow your reasoning in exaggerating your abilities. You are putting yourself in a position for trouble and a lot of nervous strain when you do that. Don't you know your employer will expect you to live up to what you said you were capable of? You would be dishonest with yourself and with your employer.

If you aren't qualified for that particular job, look for another. The only way to make work fun is to be competent for the particular job you are doing.

Apply only for jobs you know you can do well. Be honest about your age, your qualifications and the length of time you want to work. Many girls who want only summer employment will tell a prospective employer they will work permanently. He puts time and money into their training only to have them leave in a few months' time. This is not likely to give you a good recommendation for another job. Better keep it all on the up-and-up and you'll walk away with a recommendation that will help you to something better the next time.

Vonda Kay

Dear Vonda Kay,

A friend of mine works at the same place I do. She's very disrespectful to her superior and goofs off a lot. I'm afraid I'm going to get the same kind of reputation, since we work together. How can I save my job?

Janis

Dear Janis,

Yes, I suppose you will be judged, at least temporarily, by the way your friend works. However, if you don't join in on the goofing off, your good behavior may be such a contrast that it will stand out even more.

93

Do your best and don't let her laziness worry you. Bosses are pretty smart people and seem to know very well what's going on. I wouldn't do any unnecessary reporting but if you are asked about it, you are obliged to tell him.

The best way to save your job is to do it well—no employer asks more than that.

Vonda Kay

Dear Vonda Kay,

I baby-sit a lot and it's a lonely job—sitting in a strange house all evening. I want to have a friend with me, but my mother says I shouldn't. She doesn't even want me to use their phone. Isn't this a bit too strict?

Suzanne

Dear Suzanne,

Baby-sitting is a job. You are hired to do a particular thing and you get paid for it—as on any other job. And the same goes for advantages and disadvantages. On the negative side, it is lonely and the hours are often long. However, you can study; you are free to watch TV and usually even snacks are provided for you.

In turn you are expected to care for the children, to see that they are fed, bathed, put to bed or whatever the mother may ask of you. And you are responsible for what takes place in that house while the parents are out.

Long, relaxing phone chats just don't fit. Your mother is so right. There might be a change of plans or an emergency of some sort and you would have the phone tied up.

As for taking a friend, let that friend be a book and enjoy it for the evening. Few parents will leave with complete confidence if you bring someone with you.

Recognize that you are going to work. If you want a social evening, don't take a baby-sitting job.

Vonda Kay

Dear Vonda Kay,

How can one make time go faster? There are so many things I want to do, like go in the Peace Corps or work in some slum area or something, but you have to be older for everything that's interesting and I'm only fourteen.

Joannie

Dear Joannie,

Most people wish they could make time slow down, but you're looking into the future and find yourself impatient and somewhat frustrated. It's true—there are so many exciting things to do and so many people who need help.

Why don't you start in right now? Check at your local hospital. Many girls do volunteer work there. Or the YWCA—you might be able to help with the younger children, handcrafts or story hour, or games. Maybe your youth group could sponsor some special project—like an exchange with a youth group of a different background, or some clean-up program in an underprivileged area, much as the Peace Corps does.

The busier you are now, the faster time will pass for you, and the sooner you'll be old enough for the things you're dreaming about.

Vonda Kay

Dear Vonda Kay,

I am in seventh grade. I can take very good care of little kids. I like them. I want to baby-sit but my mother says I am too young. How old do you think a girl needs to be for baby-sitting?

Marcy

Dear Marcy,

There is a great deal of responsibility connected with baby-sitting. Many things can happen that require quick judgment. Every mother realizes this, because she goes through it day after day, and that just may be the reason your mother says you are too young. She may see that you are flighty, forgetful or undependable in other things and she knows that you should not be entrusted with someone's most precious possession, their children.

But there are things you can do about that. Show her that you are dependable by coming through on things she expects of you. Do your work first, then play.

You might also stop by some neighbors when they are outside with their children. Suggest watching them for a half hour or an hour while the mother does something inside the house. That way she can watch you and see how you care for her children. Maybe later, she will leave you in charge while she runs down to the store.

Probably daytime jobs are best at the beginning; seventh grade is a little young for late nighttime sitting. If you go at it slowly, I think your mother will feel you're soon ready to take a job and she'll consent to your "sitting."

Vonda Kay

8

Is College for Me?

You're going to find that I'm a real advocate of a college education. It is increasingly more important for getting a job with advancement possibilities. And more than that, it's a great time for improving your mind and capabilities and learning how to get along with people, how to make decisions and social adjustments.

But college means some hard work in high school, because entrance requirements are becoming more strict. So it's time for you to think about it very seriously and start working in that direction.

If you don't go to college, do make plans for what you want to be and do, and don't just drift into something that seems the easy way to make some money. On the basis of your preferences, take a year in secretarial school, a short course with one of the business companies that train workers for special jobs, a course given by your local hospital for practical nursing—any of these will open a job to you and you'll feel adequately prepared for it.

This is a terribly important decision. What you do the rest of your life depends on it, so take plenty of time to think it through.

Dear Vonda Kay,

My grades are all average or below. Nowadays requirements are so high for getting into college that I'm getting scared. I'm just ending my junior year so even if I tried hard, my average and class rank will be low. Should I just forget it?

Sylvia

Dear Sylvia,

No, don't "just forget it"! You still have a year ahead of you to show the high school, college—and yourself—that you can do it. If you raise your grades this last year, most colleges will take into consideration the fact that your work has improved even though your class rank is low.

You might make application to a junior college and one of the smaller colleges, too, whose requirements are not so strict. Most students who really want to go to college can find one that will accept them. Your school guidance counselor can help you secure a list of colleges and probably recommend one that is more lenient in its entrance requirements.

It's too bad, Sylvia, that you didn't wake up one year sooner and put forth the same effort that you will have to now. But it is not too late if you really have the determination to do it.

Vonda Kay

Dear Vonda Kay,

I graduate from high school at the end of this year. My folks and I have had a going row for months about where I go from here. I want to get a job. I've taken some secretarial courses, though I am in college prep classes. My grades are above average and I could easily get into college and my folks will pay for it. But I just don't want to go. I'm not interested in any more school. There's nothing that it would do for me that a job wouldn't. I want to start work as soon as school is out and become inde-

pendent. It's my life, isn't it? Why should they keep putting the pressure on for me to go to college? That's where they met and I think they've got romantic ideas about the whole thing. I'm the one in this family that's being practical. I'd surely appreciate your advice on this matter.

Linda

Dear Linda,

You are really a very fortunate girl to have parents who are eager to make college possible for you. It is a privilege to go on to college and one that many young people are begging for. You have it put right into your lap and you are debating whether to throw it out the window or not.

From my own experience, I grew up knowing that I would go to college. My parents were always interested in furthering my education and I never really considered not going. It was not that this was what was expected of me, but that this would make me a better person. So after high school I never thought of saying, "I'm as mature as I need be to face the world; my mind has developed as far as it can—I'll just hang up college and go get a job."

It's easy to understand your feelings, though—you want your independence. This is an old story. Independence is something every young person seeks, but without a proper education you are not necessarily equipped to handle the independence you strive for.

I think it's possible both to go to college and to be independent. Choose a college away from your home town, where you can't be going home too often and your family won't be visiting you. Live in a dorm with other girls your age, or perhaps if you're interested, choose a sorority house. If your parents are willing to assume your educational expenses, be grateful and let them. But get a part-time job for the extras you want, so that you won't have to ask your parents for them. Your secretarial skills should help you here.

It seems to me you are a most fortunate young lady—with

job skills, good grades and the financial backing of your parents. Don't toss this opportunity out the window.

Develop yourself. Become the kind of person you most admire and that others admire. I think that a college education is a necessary step in this direction in our day and age, and it would be a big mistake to ignore the opportunity that is yours.

Vonda Kay

Dear Vonda Kay,

I don't know how to decide what I want to be. We are supposed to write down a first, second and third choice on some forms at school. I'm only in tenth grade and I don't have any idea. How does a person decide?

Phyllis

Dear Phyllis,

It would be hard to make such a decision in the tenth grade. Even when you're in college it's often hard. Some people have taken a liberal arts major there and then decided on a specialty and taken a master's degree in their chosen field. So don't feel badly if you're having a hard time.

If I were you, I'd just think of things I enjoy doing or jobs that sound exciting—maybe an airline stewardess, a nurse or an archeologist. Put anything down on the form; it isn't binding you for life.

But during the next few years, you'd better do some serious thinking. Talk to adults about their jobs, how they like them, how they got started, what training and education it took. Read magazine articles about careers in science, teaching, the arts, and so on. You'll be discovering your own skills, and subjects that seem easier and more interesting or challenging than others. Your school will probably give aptitude tests which are helpful in directing you toward a profession suitable to your abilities.

You have time, Phyllis, just keep your grades up and your

feelers out. You'll eventually hit on the career that is just right for you.

Vonda Kay

Dear Vonda Kay,

I've been playing the cello since I was in third grade and have become quite accomplished (or so my teacher says). I'd like to go on to music school and make a career of it. Both my parents and my guidance counselor are pushing me toward another field, lab technician or something similar, since all my aptitude tests point that way. And, too, they say it is a sure job and income but my music isn't. I'm confused.

Marlene

Dear Marlene,

What a predicament! I can certainly understand your parents' feelings, but I also understand yours. Music is a wonderfully gratifying field, but, professionally, a hard one to break into.

I would recommend that you major in some other field, one that prepares you for a sure income. Minor in music. This way you'll be improving your musical abilities while you develop a wage-earning skill.

When you get out of school, if you decide to try for the big time, go to Philadelphia, New York City, or wherever you feel the best opportunities are. Audition with various symphony orchestras or television show orchestras or whatever interests you. If you make it, great! If you don't, you can support yourself while you study further and also have income during your out-of-work periods.

So many cities have their own civic orchestras where music lovers have an opportunity to perform with other skilled musicians who consider it their hobby. You can always find a place there, too, which would be a satisfaction all of your life.

Vonda Kay

101

Dear Vonda Kay,

Sometimes I wonder if the results are all worth the work. Getting an education, I mean. There are so many ways to make good money that it seems to me a real waste to put all that energy, time and money into going to school. High school is bad enough, but college? And there are plenty of jobs a guy can get and work his way up, probably make as much money by the time his class-mates get out of college as they can when they begin.

Richard

Dear Richard,

It's probably true that you could be earning very well in four years, maybe even the starting salary of a college grad. But look ahead ten years instead of four—you'll still be getting the little dollar increases while the college degree of your friends will put them in a higher income bracket.

You will have a much more secure future if you complete your education by going to college.

Is money the only basis you have for your future happiness? The broader your education, the better parent, citizen, church-man and employee or employer you'll be. You'll understand more clearly what's going on in the world and what makes people act the way they do. You'll develop new interests and broaden your personality.

Think twice, Richard, before you glibly decide to throw college out the window.

Vonda Kay

Dear Vonda Kay,

I'm not at all sure I'll like the college I'm planning to go to. I understand that you changed colleges during your four years. Would you tell me why you did and if it was a difficult change?

Sonia

102

Dear Sonia,

Yes, I did make several changes during my college career and each one was made for a definite reason.

I wanted to be near home at first, so I chose a junior college and completed my work there in a year and a half, by going to summer school. Following my graduation, I attended Northern Arizona University in Flagstaff (about 200 miles from my home). The next summer I got a job in Phoenix and because of that job I enrolled at Arizona State University. Then came my Miss America reign and my decision to go into studies involved with radio-TV. The $12,000 Miss America scholarship money made it possible for me to choose any school I wanted. I felt that UCLA offered the most in my major field, so I chose to finish my college education there.

It was not too difficult for me to make the changes because I do tend to make friends easily and was able to pick up at one school pretty nearly where I had left off at the previous one.

Becoming a part of a group of girls, as well as actively participating in organizations, is an important part of a college education. For this reason, I would recommend that you choose your college with care so you will be able to complete your four years in the same school and make a change only if it is completely necessary.

Vonda Kay

Dear Vonda Kay,

My boy friend gets mad when I even talk about having a career or some kind of job after we get married. He says he is going to take care of his wife and she isn't going to work and doesn't need any career. I don't have any special talents so I don't much care, but I do wonder sometimes if this is the way it should be.

Vicki

Dear Vicki,

I think it's wonderful for a man to feel sure he can care for his wife and give her everything she's going to need. It gives him a sense of pride to be able to do it, and every man needs that.

But I do feel there are some other considerations. There just might sometime be a crisis in your family when you would need extra income—maybe he'll want to go on to school to better his position, or you may want money for a down payment on a home or some other special need. Then you will be very glad you have some kind of vocation to turn to.

Also, as we read in so many magazine articles, many women feel a need to get out of the house and get a job when their children are all in school. This just might happen to you. It wouldn't mean your husband couldn't pay the bills, just that you feel the need of fulfillment through outside work.

I feel you should prepare for such eventualities. Even if you never use it, it is wise to have the training.

Vonda Kay

9

Decisions, Decisions—
How Do I Make Them?

You want to have fun; you want to be like the others; and you want to have self-respect and the respect of others. So how do you manage it all? You have choices to make every day. Some aren't so important on the surface, others matter a great deal, but each one gives you some experience in decision-making.

The counsel and advice of your parents and other experienced persons is very much worth listening to. It will help you think through many of your most difficult choices, yet you cannot become dependent on others for actual decisions. These you must start making for yourself.

Set goals for yourself and the kind of person you want to become. Make your decisions based on those goals. Pray about them. In the morning of each day, ask God to go with you through the day. As you are conscious of His presence beside you, there will be new light shed on each decision—and strength beyond your own to help you stick by the decisions you make.

Dear Vonda Kay,

Many of my girl friends are starting to smoke already. We're sixteen and seventeen. I haven't started it yet, but I have tried it and I must admit I kind of enjoyed it. I'm beginning to wonder if it's all that bad after all. It's something to do when we sit around and talk, and besides there's something about smoking that attracts me. Maybe it seems sophisticated or something. Some of the girls' parents don't care at all, but I think mine would hit the roof. Lots of kids sneak it till their folks get used to the idea. Do you think it's so wrong for a girl to smoke?

Katy

Dear Katy,

It's very difficult for me to see anything sophisticated about smoking. Nor do I think there is anything feminine, sweet or womanly about it. You are feeling the pressure of the crowd. One does it and all of you follow her footsteps.

I admire the girl who has the intelligence not to let herself get hooked by something she can't get out of: the girl who has the courage to say *no* when everyone else is trying it.

Katy, have you ever known an adult who was trying to stop smoking? Ask anyone who's ever tried it—it's pure agony and many just never can stop once they have the habit. And those who do make it go through weeks of desire and temptation and must fight it every minute. Why start a habit now that may someday grow stronger than you are? You're too young to make a decision that you will very likely regret. Ask any smoker you know. Practically every one will tell you he wishes he'd never started.

I can't imagine that any of you can long hide such a thing from your parents. So you had better be ready to face them. But more important than your parents' objections is your own health. Medical reports will tell you what you are doing to your body. God gave you the precious gift of life and it is your responsibility to care for that.

106

I'll never forget a young press reporter who interviewed me when I was Miss America. I think he was somewhat upset because he had to leave his cocktail outside—no liquor is permitted when Miss America is being honored. To make me look like a bit of a prude, he said rather sarcastically, "I suppose you don't smoke either."

I looked directly at him and said, "No, sir, I don't."

"Would you care to tell me why?" he asked.

I paused and asked if he was sure he wanted my answer. He nodded, so I told him. "I believe my body is the temple of the Holy Spirit—that's what the Bible says—and believing that, I wouldn't smoke."

Well, Katy, you asked and I've told you. What are you going to do about it?

Vonda Kay

Dear Vonda Kay,

Cheating is a real problem at my school. I'm not tempted to get help for myself, but what do I do when someone asks me? They're good friends. They know I make good grades and know the answers. I don't want them to think I'm a prude, but what . . . ?

Kerry

Dear Kerry,

There are *two* ways to cheat—one is to look at someone else's answers and the other is to give them yours. You may as well face it: both are dishonest. Being considered a prude is no fun, but living with a bad conscience isn't either. Try to explain ahead of time to the friends who sit near you that you feel sharing answers is neither fair nor right. Offer to study with them, share your class notes or help them in any way you can before the test, but don't compromise your standard of honesty. No

107

really considerate friend will ask this of you when he or she understands how you feel about it.

Vonda Kay

Dear Vonda Kay,
   Is there any real danger in experimenting, just experimenting, with things like glue sniffing, maybe getting drunk—just once, even the reefers and other stuff that some of the guys are passing around? I'm not the kind of guy that would get hooked and I do think everyone should know about such things, don't you?

Steve

Dear Steve,
   Can't you find all you need to know by reading what the authorities say about it? I suppose some rather stupid people would experiment with a stick of dynamite—just an experiment so they'd know how dangerous it really is.
   Why must you get burned just to "know about these things"? Let someone who is hooked tell you. Or someone who has gone through a "withdrawal" when every cell in his body was calling for more.
   No one can possibly know when he first tries liquor, drugs or any other habit-forming thing, if he is the one who will get "hooked." Stay away. There are some things you can learn from the experience of others, not your own, and this is one of them.

Vonda Kay

Dear Vonda Kay,
   It's something of a fad in our school to see what you can pick up in the stores without getting caught. Mostly it's just make-up and costume jewelry, but some of the girls are lifting sweaters and really nice things. They tell their mothers that they borrowed them from a friend. They brag about it at school. Many of their parents are really fine, respected folks in town and it would kill

108

them to know, but they'd sure soon put a stop to it. Should I do anything about it or just keep my trap shut?

Dorothy

Dear Dorothy,

I have read that shop-lifting is becoming a major problem in department stores and teen-agers are the biggest culprits. You may call it a "fad" or "lifting" or any other name, but it is still stealing. Besides breaking the law, it is damaging each girl's sense of right and wrong. The longer they get away with it, the worse it is for them.

Have you tried talking to them about it? I think you should try that first, explaining the loss it means to the store, and help them to be aware of the consequences and disgrace if they are caught— and sooner or later they will be.

If that doesn't work, talk it over with your mother. Perhaps she could drop hints to their mothers that would wake them up concerning their daughters' actions. Maybe some trusted teacher could help reason with the girls.

It's awkward for you, I can see, and you don't want to be a "squealer," but this is wrong and you have a certain obligation to yourself and your friends. Better act quickly before they get into real trouble.

Vonda Kay

Dear Vonda Kay,

What should a girl (that's me) do if she doesn't like off-color jokes (and I don't) and someone tells one in her presence? I don't like to act square or anything, but I'm always uncomfortable.

Lynne

Dear Lynne,

If it's possible to leave the group where such a story is being told, just say, "Excuse me, please," and do so. If not, and you are asked why you don't laugh, simply reply that you don't find that kind of joke humorous. Sometimes, before a story is told, you are asked if you want to hear a joke. Answer honestly, "Yes, if it's a good one; no, if it's dirty." Just forget about being a square. In the end you will earn the respect of your friends—and they'll admire you for your courage.

Vonda Kay

Dear Vonda Kay,

I wish I knew how to set standards of right and wrong. It seems like I get a clear idea and then something happens that gets me all mixed up. All kinds of things, like use of money, obeying my parents (even when they're unreasonable), how I act with my boy friend. You know what I mean? It's kind of hard to explain, but is there a way to always know what is right and what is wrong? Do you think my parents always know? Even the minister?

Donna

Dear Donna,

I would doubt if anyone can give you a clear-cut formula for right and wrong. We often hear our friends, both old and young, say, "I hope I did the right thing." As for your parents and the minister—I imagine that they aren't always so sure either, though their years of experience certainly equip them to make decisions with a great deal of wisdom and their counsel should be helpful to you.

There are three suggestions I would make to you. First, maybe if you would decide on the kind of person you want to be, you could base your decisions on the answer to the question, "What would that kind of person do in this situation?" If you can separate yourself just a little from the situation, you may be able to weigh the problem more carefully.

Secondly, I believe that you probably know basically what is right and what is wrong and what things are on the borderline. The training you've had in your home, church and school has prepared you for this. You've been taught about honesty, about consideration of other people, about your own health, and so many other things that are really basics in decision-making. Try very hard to look at each question honestly and if you need help, go to someone whose own character recommends him to you as one who could help.

Finally, look to the finest example in all the world for your best answer. Jesus always knew what was right and wrong. If you study His teachings and example, you will find the most perfect standard of conduct. Try asking yourself, "What would Jesus do?" You'll see the problem more clearly and come up with an answer that will put you on the right road for happiness and certainty.

Vonda Kay

Dear Vonda Kay,

How do you make yourself study when there are so many more interesting things to do? Even when I do sit down to study, my mind wanders off to boys, clothes, and everything but the book before me. My grades are hurting.

Bev

Dear Bev,

Believe me, your problem is not unique. In fact, it's a question I'd probably have asked of you or anyone who would have shown interest in discussing it. The funny thing is that we *can* concentrate on the interesting things—a ball game, a movie (even two or three hours without interruption), a phone conversation. Of course, they seem more interesting than studying—but concentrating on them proves it can be done.

The solution I've worked out requires a certain amount of discipline, but it has helped me.

Set a goal for yourself in each class when you first start out the term or semester. Say to yourself, "In this class I am capable of making a B." In another, an A. Maybe aim a little higher than what you think you'll do, so you really have something to work toward. When you sit down to study, remember your goal as your mind starts to wander. Be determined to conquer the situation.

Where do you do your studying? Find a place that has no distractions, even if you have to set up a card table in the basement. Make a schedule for use of your study time, like chemistry from seven to eight, history eight-fifteen to nine-fifteen, etc. Get the most difficult subjects out of the way first, or break up the study time with something that's easier for you. After you read for fifteen or twenty minutes, go back and recap in your mind what you've read in order to make sure it's sticking.

Stopping a wandering mind takes discipline and lots of it. You are the only one who can remedy the situation. And I hope you do raise those grades!

Vonda Kay

Dear Vonda Kay,

Some of my friends and I were talking about how to say no. Why is it so much harder to say no than yes? Like not wanting to accept some invitation but you're afraid you'll hurt someone's feelings if you don't. Or how to say no when your date or the other kids are going somewhere that you know is out of bounds for you. It's always such an awkward situation.

Dear Tina,

You are so right. I know it is difficult to say no. I am asked to speak before youth groups and conferences almost every weekend. I want to accept each one because I consider it a real opportunity, but I know that physically I just can't handle that along with my studies and everything else. So I've had to learn to say no, but with sincere regret.

To tell the truth, Tina, I'm glad that you even *want* to say no in certain situations. So many girls would rather just compromise their standards than find the way to say no. No one wants to be considered a spoil-sport or be labeled a goody-goody, nor do you want to hurt somebody's feelings.

The easiest and simplest way to say no is just: "I'm sorry, but I'm not coming." Don't sound hesitant or you're in for an argument. And don't add a lie (call it white if you like—it's still a lie). If you don't want to give a reason for not doing something, don't let it sound as if you are superior to the others—they will resent that—just state the fact. "I'm going someplace with my parents, but thanks anyway."

Now, how to turn down an invitation, maybe a date or a party you don't want to attend. You're fortunate if you already have plans, but don't make some up. That always sounds fake. Just say, "Thanks so much, but I just can't."

It isn't easy and I know it. How many times have you heard adults say, "I just couldn't say no to her, so I promised I'd serve on the committee," and then complain about it for days because they didn't really want to do it. If you say yes under pressure, you're almost always sorry and it's harder to get out of it later. Better to be honest in the beginning. Honest—and courteous.

Vonda Kay

Dear Vonda Kay,

A girl in my junior class had to get married. She is being tutored at home till her baby comes, so she is out of school activities. She's really a nice kid but the rest of us don't know quite how we

should act. Should we invite her to join us like she used to?
Would she feel awkward? We wonder, too, if we would get a
bad name. She must be lonely and terribly sorry about the mess
she's made of things.

Anne

Dear Anne,

I'm sure, too, that your friend must be a very lonely person and I think you are thoughtful to want to include her. Certainly you could invite her to join you in all-girl activities. I think it would be awkward to include her in mixed groups, more so for the boys than for you girls, but she would surely be the first to understand and accept that. Call her up and drop by to see her. Maybe she'd like to talk about school work and know where you are in certain subjects in order to keep up. This is a time of testing when she'll find out who her real friends are and I would guess she's being hurt plenty.

Jesus was very kind to the woman who was accused of adultery and, in His own wise way, turned away the angry, judging mob. This is a lesson for all of us and I believe you should not let what she has done keep you from being her friend.

There may be a few people who stand ready to throw stones— at her and at you. Don't worry about getting a bad reputation yourself by being a friend to someone who needs you, as long as you know that you are being the right kind of person. Actually, I suppose Jesus didn't have a very good reputation among some of the people because He associated with sinners, and yet He is certainly the most perfect example you could follow. Forgiveness and love work wonders in a life and they can mean so much to the person who receives them.

Vonda Kay

Dear Vonda Kay,

I have just accepted a diamond from a fellow I have gone with for over a year. He's a wonderful person, has a good job, is kind and loving and our families know and like each other.

We're starting to talk wedding plans and where we'll live and all that goes with marriage. But sometimes I seem to get scared, and have questions about whether this is right and whether it will work out. It's such a terribly important step.

How did you know the man you married was the right one? Didn't you ever have doubts about what you were doing?

Liz

Dear Liz,

A few years ago I think I would have answered you very glibly, "If there is *any* doubt, then he is probably not the right one." Now I know that you should study your doubts and see where they seem to originate. If they concern really deep-down important goals and standards, things you know you could never get used to nor be able to spend a lifetime with, then you should consider your relationship very carefully; your doubts are probably warning signs. Don't ever count on the marriage vow to change his friends or habits. Decide how important are the negative things you see in him in comparison to the things you love about him.

You asked me how I knew for sure—well, if I had any doubts, they were so overshadowed by the wonderful things about the man I had chosen to marry that they quickly faded into the background. I feel that you must respect and admire the man you marry, as well as love him. It's important that you have a number of common interests and ideas and yet have your own individual ideas and interests—both help in making a successful marriage. Sharing a common religious faith is most important.

I suppose it's natural to question just a little, or maybe it's more that you are a little frightened at the idea of leaving your family behind and about your own capabilities as a wife and homemaker. I think you can doubt too much about marriage—some people scare themselves right out of it. It's not something to fear, but the most wonderful part of life. And it's amazing how, when two people feel real love and concern for each other, they can work out the little irritations that arise. It takes consideration on both sides to do it.

I guess I'd sum it up by saying that if your doubts are stronger than your love for the man, then you had better take a little more time to make this terribly important decision. Spend some of that time in prayer. I feel that this is very important. Such a big step, probably the biggest one of your life, should be one of prayerful consideration and seeking of God's guidance.

And I wish you much happiness.

Vonda Kay

10

I Have Some Questions
and Doubts About Religion . . .

Along with all the other questions you ask of me, there are many concerning the church, God, faith and your feelings about religion.

Just as you question everything else, it is natural and probably very good that you should be questioning in this area, too. Don't ever be afraid or ashamed of asking questions. Where you come out is the important thing, and your goal should be for a deeper, stronger faith.

If you seek in honesty and with a desire for a closer relationship to God, you will come out stronger and better for it. Find people you can talk with as these questions come to you. Evaluate the things you hear, the things you read, and the things you've always been taught, continuing always to ask God for light and guidance.

Dear Vonda Kay,

I'm bothered about my feelings in church and I'm afraid to tell my folks how I feel. I go every Sunday but I just sit there and don't feel a thing. My mind wanders off and never comes back. It's really a waste of time for me, but I can't tell my folks that. Would you say I should keep going, or should I stand up to my folks and tell them I'm just not going any more?

Dick

Dear Dick,

No, I don't think you should tell your folks you aren't going to church any more. Church services are important to your spiritual growth just as school is to your intellectual growth.

I suppose there are many things that can prevent a person from really worshipping. Perhaps you don't particularly like the minister and for that reason aren't interested in what he has to say. Maybe you don't like the order of the service and find it boring.

Well, let me tell you something. When you say your mind wanders and you feel it's a waste of time, there are other people who feel the same way but don't have the nerve to admit it. Sometimes I will come away from church wondering if I really got anything out of the service that morning. But one thing I do have is the satisfaction of knowing that I took an hour out of my week to worship God. Perhaps the minister wasn't up to par, or the music not what I would have chosen, and maybe the order of service is getting a little humdrum, but at least I gave an hour of the week to God, one hour of the whole week—and surely that's not too much for anyone to do. We should be grateful to the church for providing an opportunity to worship.

I believe it would help, too, if instead of just one hour on Sunday, you would get interested in the youth group activities. Other Christian activities in a Christ-centered atmosphere are important. The fun and fellowship with other young people will carry over into your attitudes toward church.

Vonda Kay

Dear Vonda Kay,

I went forward at a youth meeting. I felt all happy and really wanted to follow Jesus. Back in school and at home, I lost that happy feeling. Things seem so ordinary. No one else seems to feel that way. Now I wonder if it was right to say I accepted Christ.

Sherry

Dear Sherry,

You are the only one who can say if you accepted Christ or not. That decision is a big one, for it may mean changing many parts of your life. However, I hope you don't get discouraged just because you don't have that joyous feeling you had at the moment of your decision.

Life is made up of valleys and hilltops and you will have to walk them both. Just be assured that Christ is there with you, and if you recognize His presence, you are sure to find joy.

I hope you have joined some Christian youth group or have found some Christian young people to associate with. The fellowship, understanding and sharing of experiences that come from being with like-minded friends is really wonderful and would probably help you in your time of doubting.

Surely some pastor or youth leader is following through with you on your decision to accept Christ. If no one is, do try to find a minister or some devoted adult to whom you can talk occasionally. All of us need guidance at times, but those who are new in faith need it even more.

Vonda Kay

Dear Vonda Kay,

What do you think of a girl who joined a certain church just because a boy she wants to impress goes there?

Amy

Dear Amy,

Without knowing more of the circumstances involved, it is difficult to say. At least she has joined the church and is probably attending regularly, even if she's doing it to impress a boy.

I think her initial reason is not a good one, but it just might be the means to leading her to Christ. Your criticism of her is a poor Christian testimony on your part—and I somehow suspect that the same boy may be the basis of that, which doesn't make *you* much better, does it?

I wonder what she is thinking about the people she's found in your church—does she see anything different in them? Does she see people whom she would like to pattern her life after? Are they warm and friendly? These questions are much more important and they are the ones you should be asking—and answering.

Vonda Kay

Dear Vonda Kay,

I don't think the church has much place in the lives of modern teen-agers. It's so stiff and formal and our generation is frank, informal and open. Is it the church or us?

Vi

Dear Vi,

I think you are misjudging the church when you say it is stiff and formal. There are so many changes taking place within the church, and ministers are seeking ways to make worship and their sermons more real and applicable to you and to all others who come. Are you sure you're not going with a closed mind?

Even if the morning service seems formal to you, there are always youth activities and discussions and study groups. That's just the place you should be open and frank and ask questions. You'll find others like you and you can share your feelings in honesty.

I believe it is important for a teen-ager to associate with the church. That is the place to go for answers that mean something. It is also the place to make lasting friendships, the kind that help you grow in Christ and His love.

Don't judge the church, for it is made up of people just like you. Take a look at yourself to see where improvements can be made.

Vonda Kay

Dear Vonda Kay,

My oldest sister has two little boys. They are both little dolls. They come over to our house often and all of us love them so much. We have just learned that the younger one has leukemia.

It's almost too awful to think about what the next months will mean to the little guy. My sister is very brave and says, "God's will be done." I can't understand how she can say that or even think that God would want him to die. How do you think a person should face death and what do you think God is doing?

Laurie

Dear Laurie,

My heart really goes out to you as you face the coming months and even more as you try to think through this whole business of life and death and God.

First of all, even while you're confused and afraid, please don't let either your little nephew or your sister know it. They need your strength, too. Make every minute of his life happy and joyous for him. Enjoy him and let him enjoy life. Be thankful for every moment that you do have him with you, and make each moment count toward happiness for everyone in your family.

I wonder if anyone can answer your question, "What is God doing?" It is very hard sometimes to know what God's will is and you are going through just such a time. You are right: probably God wouldn't wish anything like this on a little one.

But perhaps what your sister means by "God's will" being done is that His will may be done in helping all the family to accept the situation, to help all of you to come out stronger Christians and perhaps be drawn closer to the Lord.

Try to seek God's will for you personally during this trying experience. It can be a time for you to mature in unselfish love. You'll discover that many people are praying for him and that will strengthen you.

And don't you stop praying. Miracles happen every day. Remember the verse, "God is our refuge and our strength, a very present help in time of trouble."

Vonda Kay

Dear Vonda Kay,

Seems like the world is in an awful mess and I get all discouraged about it. What's the point in trying hard to do something or be somebody if it's all going to blow up?

Layne

Dear Layne,

It's interesting that you should express your feelings of concern about what's going on in the world, because my husband and I were discussing almost the same thing the other night. He reminded me of something that seemed particularly helpful and explains a little why today's world seems so much worse than yesterday's. Maybe it will give you something to think about, too.

It used to take several days or a week for news stories to make it from the point of happening to American newspaper headlines. Even radio stations weren't able to get the news on the air immediately; it was often 12 to 16 hours old.

But now we see news as it's being made. We can watch our American servicemen in action in Vietnam almost at the moment of battle. From London, dignitaries debate with U.S. Congressmen by way of satellite. We see pictures taken on the moon, right after they've been shot; we watch the launching of space-ships; we see people shot before our very eyes.

Our systems of communication have improved so incredibly that we have become increasingly aware of the problems of the world. The problems have always been there, and many people lived through them and made something of themselves in spite of them. It's just that the people in one part of the world were not aware of what was occurring in another part.

The world may "blow up" tomorrow, or it may go on for a long, long time. It will probably still be going when you are in a position to do something about some part of its troubles. Why don't you dig in, learn all you can about what's going on and why, and prepare yourself to remedy some little corner of the confusion you find?

Vonda Kay

Dear Vonda Kay,

I've been raised in a Christian home. We always have gone to church and said grace before meals. We try to apply Christian principles to our conduct and often discuss it. I love my family and the way we get along and really like each other. So why would I have doubts about my faith and religion and prayer and God? Sometimes I get to thinking that prayer is just therapy and I get along fine, with or without. The church service seems all phony to me and like people are putting on a big act, standing up and sitting down, saying a creed or prayer in unison. And God—well, if I were to be honest, I guess I'd say, "Who needs him?" Now I feel almost sinful thinking all these things, but there isn't any proof of God or of answers to prayer. Who ever knows whether the outcome would have happened anyway, prayer or no? I talk with my folks sometimes about this, but we don't make much real contact. I hate to have them quote Scripture to me, because what does that prove? Maybe the Bible isn't the final word either.

It seems funny to see this down on paper. You'll probably think I'm a lost creature, but I'm really a very happy person, well

123

behaved, high idealism, service minded and all that. I guess I just feel that I'm equipped to handle life's problems, and talking to the air about them doesn't make sense. I don't know why this has happened to me—I know that lots of my friends feel the same way, but they won't tell their parents or talk about it in youth meetings. Is there an answer?

Jan

Dear Jan,

I'd be the last person to criticize you for raising the questions you do. I too have found myself questioning what my parents taught me and the things I learn at church—or even why I went to church. The wonderful thing about questioning is that it leads you to seek answers. Many times young people completely accept their parents' religion and beliefs and learn to say all the answers. But they need to believe it, feel it and understand it for themselves. Your doubts put you on the starting line of a genuine search for a more meaningful religious experience in Christ.

I wish I could offer you positive answers to every question you have raised, but faith just can't be proved with words. This you must find on your own and for yourself. Remember, without a question and a questioning mind there would be no answers, so you may be off to a very good start.

And God—who needs Him, you ask. I, for one. During my most serious questioning, I turned to Him and found that I came out with a stronger, really truer faith. He is very real, even if some people don't believe it and others think of Him in a very immature way.

I'm afraid there are many people who would disagree with you about "answered prayer," for the greatest answer is a richer fellowship with God and there are so many people who have found that. Then, too, prayers may seem unanswered from our very limited viewpoint, when they are being answered in a much wiser way in God's great understanding and love. We need to remember, too, that prayer isn't all asking for things; there's some listening to it.

Really, I'm no theologian. I can only testify how much Christ means to me, and He means so very much. You say you appreciate your home and family and the love you share: did you ever stop to think that it's your parents' love of God and their faith in His leading that has made it so?

Please, Jan, keep searching for answers. Don't get cynical or lose contact with the best Friend you'll ever have.

Vonda Kay